Questioning ?Performance

The director's essential guide to health, safety and the environment

David Eves and the
Rt Hon John Gummer

Publisher's note

© IOSH Services Ltd, 2005
Revised and reprinted 2007, 2008, 2009, 2010, 2011
Printed in England by the Lavenham Press

ISBN 978 0 901357 37 3

Contents

Preface

Directors should always have understood that the health and safety of employees was an important part of their responsibilities. Yet, in the past, these were issues that too many boards assumed could largely be delegated to others and needed little of their direct input. Today, that attitude can no longer be sustained. Not only has the law increasingly insisted on the direct liability of all company directors for these matters, but the media and public opinion are pressing for an ever more stringent approach.

Indeed, the scope of those responsibilities has been steadily growing, as the principles of corporate responsibility have widened, demanding that directors take account of the effects their companies have on the wider environment. Producer responsibility and the concept that the polluter should pay now form the basis of a whole raft of law that applies both in Britain and across Europe and beyond. Even though many of us would want to see significant simplification and increased clarity in all this lawmaking, it is clearly a proper duty of a company director to ensure the protection of those who work in his company and the customers and suppliers who visit its premises.

Nor can that duty stop at the factory gates or the office reception. The more we understand about the environmental challenges – whether global issues like climate change or local concerns of watercourse pollution – the more we have to accept the challenge to reduce our emissions, improve our systems and minimise our waste. It is not just that we ought to do this for the general good: it also makes good business sense to produce more from less, by cutting our costs by cutting our waste, energy and water consumption, and reducing loss of time through accident and illness.

No director can ignore the risk to the reputation of his company and its brand that health and safety and environmental expectations present. Like it or not, customers, shareholders, commentators and lawmakers expect ever higher standards of all of us and exact a high price if we fail.

This book is therefore very timely. It sets out, in a direct and easily digested way, the legal responsibilities and public expectations of company directors for safety, health and the environment. Armed with this, a company director can feel assured that he knows how properly to cover these important elements of his responsibilities. It fulfils a long-felt want and I am particularly pleased to commend it.

Sir Nigel Rudd
Non-executive chairman of BAA and Pendragon plc
Deputy chairman of Barclays
Non-executive director of Sappi SpA and BAE Systems

About the authors

David Eves CB is an Honorary Vice-President of IOSH and an Honorary Fellow of the IIRSM. Formerly Deputy Director General and HM Chief Inspector in the HSE, he is Vice-President of Safety Groups UK, an ambassador for NEBOSH and an external examiner at the University of Warwick School of Law. He has worked as a consultant in the private sector, served as Secretary General and Technical Adviser to the International Association of Labour Inspection and has been co-opted to the CIEH's Policy Development Board and RoSPA's National Occupational Safety and Health Committee. He has worked in health and safety for 45 years.

Lord Deben, formerly the Rt Hon John Gummer MP, is chairman of Sancroft International Ltd, a consultancy specialising in corporate social responsibility issues. He is a former Secretary of State for the Environment, Minister for Agriculture, Fisheries and Food, and Minister for Health and Safety at Work. He was Member of Parliament for Suffolk Coastal until May 2010.

Introduction

This book helps directors sleep at night. It tells them, clearly and succinctly, what they need to know and do to control losses and fulfil their responsibilities towards their workforce, their shareholders and society. It is not intended to be a manual for the professional health and safety practitioner or environmental risk manager, for whom there are many sources of technical advice. Nor is it a legal textbook. Its purpose is simply to help busy directors and senior managers, who may not be experts in these fields, understand their responsibilities and fulfil them by knowing how to ask their advisers and managers the right questions and to recognise the right answers.

Good companies increasingly recognise good management of risks to health and safety at work and the environment as vital to the success of their business. It has become an essential feature of the corporate social responsibility* (CSR) agenda. Insurers, institutional investors and fund managers are beginning to ask searching questions about performance in these areas, seeing them as key indicators of a company's ability to manage the business well.

Injuries and ill health caused by work cost the UK economy up to £36 billion a year, including loss of production, cost of medical treatment, administrative costs, compensation and insurance payments, and damage to property. Put another way, these costs equate to nearly 10 per cent of company trading profits. Catastrophic failures of health and safety management in recent years have damaged and even destroyed some company reputations.

---

* CSR can be defined as 'a system whereby organisations integrate social and environmental concerns into their business operations and interactions with stakeholders' (IOSH: *Systems in focus*, Wigston, 2003).

Concern about environmental management is growing as the causes of climate change begin to be better understood.

Business has to cope with an increasing regulatory burden but there are other, compelling reasons why directors need to take their responsibilities very seriously. Breaches of laws protecting safety, health and the environment are regarded as criminal offences in the UK, Europe and elsewhere in the world. After a chemical plant disaster at Bhopal killed over 2,000 people in 1984, a warrant was issued for the arrest of the chairman of the international company concerned should he ever set foot in India again. Directors have legal liabilities, and individuals as well as companies may be prosecuted if they are negligent of their duties.

In addition to the risk to individual directors, companies themselves face heavy penalties. Seven-figure fines for breaches of health and safety and environmental law are not unheard of. There is increasing pressure for both individuals and companies to face manslaughter charges when management failures cause deaths at work. The media take great interest in such matters and are quick to lay blame and pillory corporate failure. Society looks for retribution, while the regulators publish annual lists of convictions to name and shame transgressors. The risk of damage to company reputations when serious incidents occur is now much higher than in the past, and a poor track record is likely to affect investment decisions adversely and to cause grave harm to the business.

The Corporate Manslaughter and Corporate Homicide Act 2007 aims to address difficulties in securing convictions of larger organisations by replacing the requirement to prove a 'controlling mind' with one of establishing management failure that constitutes a gross breach of the organisation's duty of care, resulting in death.

Part 1 of this book explains the principles of health and safety and environmental regulation applying in the UK, setting out the responsibilities and duties of directors. It provides insights into British regulatory strategy and attitudes towards enforcement, and also gives a European and global perspective for companies operating internationally.

Good practice in health, safety and environmental management is described, based on real, practical experience of what successful companies have been able to achieve, rather than on theory alone. The book discusses the key features of a company health, safety and environment policy, the processes of risk assessment and environmental impact assessment and control, and the principal elements in effective systems of health and safety and environmental management. It goes on to address major hazards: this chapter will be of particular interest to directors who are responsible for sites and operations attracting the regulatory requirements for safety cases and major hazard controls for safety and the environment under the Seveso Directives and the Control of Major Accident Hazards (COMAH) Regulations.

It also explains how performance can be measured, and the use of key performance indicators. It suggests ways of ensuring that the board receives the necessary assurance for the purposes of corporate governance and gives the necessary commitment and leadership to its staff, so as to achieve the benefits of a positive culture.

Each chapter concludes with references to relevant legislation and guidance, which can usually be obtained via the websites of the regulatory authorities concerned or from the Stationery Office.

Part 2 provides a ready reference 'A to Z' of commonly encountered occupational hazards, the kind of control measures that are likely to be appropriate and some issues coming over the horizon. It is not intended to provide encyclopaedic legal or technical information. Instead, the aim is to help the director with relatively little knowledge of these issues to ask searching questions about whether the company has identified the significant hazards in its business, has assessed the risks properly and has introduced the appropriate controls.

Part 3 contains appendices dealing with subjects including recent disasters, Employers' Liability Compulsory Insurance, key facts and figures, useful sources of information, legislation, and a glossary of common terms.

In our work as directors of the Sancroft Group we specialise in advising companies on corporate responsibility issues. *Questioning performance* is the result of that experience, in addition to the decades of knowledge and know-how we have accrued in our respective careers. It is intended to help directors of companies committed to CSR to improve their health, safety and environmental management performance. They will thereby be better able to manage risk, improve profitability, and protect their reputation and brand.

David Eves and John Gummer
London
November 2005

Part 1
Management matters

Chapter 1
What health and safety law demands

"As a society, we have increased expectations that regulations can and will protect consumers, businesses, workers and the environment, coupled with an increasing need to keep our businesses efficient and flexible to face new competitive challenges. Our regulatory system has the pivotal role in resolving the regular conflict between prosperity and protection." *Sir Philip Hampton, The Hampton Review, 2005*

Health and safety law in Great Britain requires employers to protect their employees and other members of the public from the risks associated with the enterprise that they run. These duties are extensive and the penalties for neglecting them can be very severe. Yet most people think only of financial responsibilities when they consider the duties of directors. Their responsibilities under health and safety law seem less well understood.

Despite that, most managers and directors would want to ensure that they protect their workforce from sickness and danger, recognise the damage done to a firm's reputation by a bad record in safety, and would be horrified if they thought their company was actively endangering life and limb.

The reason for the disconnection is that directors tend to assume that the management has got it all covered or that their particular company really doesn't have any issues as their employees work largely in offices. But these matters cannot be left to chance or to others. A board director has a principal duty under the Health and Safety at Work etc Act 1974 to ensure, so far as is reasonably practicable, the health, safety and welfare of all employees. He or she must also conduct the undertaking in such a way as to ensure, so far as is reasonably practicable, that people who are not employees, including members of the public, are not exposed to risks from the activities of the business.

These are sometimes referred to as the 'general duties'. Together with the requirements of regulations made under the Act, at the very minimum they mean:

- making the workplace safe and without risks to health
- ensuring that plant and machinery are safe and that safe systems of work are set and followed
- keeping dust, fumes and noise under control
- ensuring that articles and substances are stored, moved and used safely
- providing adequate welfare facilities
- giving employees the information, instruction, training and supervision necessary for their health and safety
- providing free any protective clothing or equipment required by law
- reporting certain injuries, diseases and dangerous occurrences to the enforcing authority
- providing adequate first aid facilities
- consulting a safety representative (or worker representative), if one has been appointed, about matters affecting employees' health and safety
- setting up a safety committee if asked to do so by safety representatives.

The 'workplace' may be anywhere that employees work, such as a site, shop floor or office. Plant and equipment will include not simply heavy machinery in factories but also the IT equipment used in offices and shops. It means organising workplaces like offices so that work can be done without the problems of musculoskeletal disorders, repetitive strain injuries, eye strain and issues associated with working with computers.

Directors have other safety-related duties as well – for example under fire legislation to take precautions against fire, including provision of adequate means of escape, of fighting the fire and of raising the alarm. If you are a designer, manufacturer, importer or supplier of articles and substances you also have duties to supply information about them and help ensure safety in their use.

In addition to these general requirements there are further more specific duties that may apply, such as those that concern work in confined spaces, taking precautions against danger from electrical equipment, ensuring that lifts, lifting equipment, steam boilers and the like are kept safely maintained and regularly examined, and so on. These are usually covered by specific Regulations made under the 1974 Act or by Codes of Practice.

Rightly, employees have responsibilities too. Essentially they must take reasonable care of themselves and anyone who may be affected by their 'acts or omissions'. They must co-operate with you to enable you to comply with the law, and they must not interfere with anything you provide for their health, safety and welfare.

All this seems perfectly sensible. So why is complying with health and safety law widely thought to be so difficult? Part of the explanation is a matter of history. In place of the old-fashioned rules, the 1974 Act tried to move to a system that would encourage a culture of safety at work. Thereby it began a process of modernisation and simplification of the law. This followed the recommendations of the Robens Committee which had examined the factors behind the deteriorating safety performance that had been so noticeable in Great Britain during the 1960s.

The creation of these 'general duties' radically altered the approach to safety regulation. It introduced goal-setting requirements to replace the outdated prescriptive, specific, rigid and *ad hoc* requirements of previous safety legislation – particularly the Factories Acts.

It meant that employers were no longer told what to do to comply with the law but had choices to make. The new law's aim was to involve employers in the process of managing safety. Instead of insisting that they follow a set of rules, they were required to take an active part in assessing and countering the risks inherent in their businesses. The general responsibility to ensure the proper control of risks to the health and safety of workers and the public was clearly visited on employers. How they decided to fulfil that obligation was left largely up to them.

Many firms have found this very challenging and would have preferred a more prescriptive approach. They want to know exactly where they stand. But Parliament's challenge to employers in making the 1974 Act was deliberate. This was not meant to be a sterile imposition of a series of rules but a means of involving employers in making their workplaces a safe environment. The Act was intended to force continuous improvement while allowing innovation and technological advance to continue. The more flexible goal-setting approach provides for the active involvement of employers in finding the best way to establish a healthy and safe working environment. It therefore involves more than handing down a series of prescriptive rules. However, the responsibilities are limited to what it would be sensible to require a company to do.

That is why the general duties set out in the 1974 Act are qualified by the phrase 'so far as is reasonably practicable' (sometimes referred to by regulators and academics as 'SFAIRP'). Even this can be a source of misunderstanding of the meaning of the duties in British health and safety law. Its use has been the subject of a challenge by the European Commission, which was heard and rejected by the European Court. However construed, the expression certainly does not allow a cop-out. Unless the time, trouble, cost and difficulty involved in eliminating or reducing a risk are grossly disproportionate to that risk, then it must be removed or controlled (see *Edwards v National Coal Board*).

This is a balanced judgment for employers to make, and must be based on proper assessment of the risk (see Chapter 5). Other similar expressions you may hear in the context of risk management are 'as low as reasonably practicable' (ALARP) and 'as low as reasonably achievable' (ALARA).

The concept of SFAIRP is also important to implementing the wider demands of sustainable development. It is increasingly recognised that our society must learn to grow in a way that does not lay unacceptable burdens on other people here or in the rest of the world nor on future generations. That, of course, is sooner said than done. Drilling down from high-flown generalities to practical action is a complex business. It does, however, mean that we measure the risks of our actions and activities and seek to minimise them. It also means that such assessment must become part of the way we live and work, built into all decision making, and constantly updated and reconsidered.

In that way, good practice is what is reasonably practicable, and what is reasonably practicable will change with new technology, more information and improved ways of working. Therefore, the director cannot rely on a single assessment of risk but has to be sure that there is a culture of continuous improvement and a process for encouraging and applying new insights and understanding.

That is why the expression 'so far as is reasonably practicable' applies a proportionate approach to risk control. It avoids setting prescriptive standards that would freeze technological progress, while at the same time insisting that, where it is reasonably practicable to reduce risks further, this should be done. It is a powerful driver for change and improvement and it reduces the number of occasions when we can legitimately argue that the regulations do not properly take individual circumstances into account nor keep up with changes in techniques and practices.

These 'general duties' have for 30 years been the bedrock of health and safety practice but were given greater definition and made more specific in the Management of Health and Safety at Work Regulations (often referred to as the 'Management Regulations'). Originally introduced in 1992 to implement the European Framework Directive of 1989, they were revised in 1999.

The effect of these important regulations is to make more specific the steps that employers have to take in order to comply with the general duties already laid down in the 1974 Act. In this way the process by which directors must ensure that they carry out their responsibilities is made more precise. They are required to:

- assess risks faced by employees and others not in their employment
- make effective arrangements for planning, organising, controlling, monitoring and reviewing preventive and protective measures
- appoint one or more 'competent persons' to help in undertaking measures needed to comply with the law
- provide employees with comprehensible and relevant information about the risks they face and the risk control measures.

This all provides a framework within which a proper health and safety culture may grow. Today, that framework is being further revised to take account of new concerns about corporate governance and to seek to reverse the slowdown in health and safety improvement.

How the health and safety regulator works

There are particular reasons why health and safety should now be climbing up the agenda. In 2000 the UK government was becoming concerned that the improving trend in accidents and ill health had stalled. It therefore launched two new strategies: 'Revitalising health and safety at work' and 'Securing health together'. These set national targets for improvement by 2010, aiming to:

- reduce the incidence rate (the number per 100,000 workers) of working days lost through work-related injury and ill health by 30 per cent
- reduce the incidence rate of fatal and major injury accidents by 10 per cent
- reduce the incidence rate of cases of work-related ill health by 20 per cent.

Half of the intended improvement was to have been achieved by 2004 and the government gave the Health and Safety Commission (HSC) the task of ensuring that those targets were met.

The HSC was originally set up under the 1974 Act as a tripartite body on which government, employers and trade unions were represented. Later, other members were added to represent wider public interests. The HSC set the overall aims and objectives, while its day-to-day functions were carried out by the separate Health and Safety Executive (HSE). This model became outdated and in 2008 the HSC and HSE merged into a single national regulatory body, known simply as the Health and Safety Executive. (Readers will find references to the HSC later in the book where they remain historically correct.)

When achieving half the required targets by 2004 proved illusory, the HSC published a new 'Strategy for workplace health and safety to 2010 and beyond' in the hope of achieving those targets at a later date. Its key features were:

- focusing HSE resources on poor performance to get best results
- promoting greater worker involvement, recognising that staff and managers are best placed to make workplaces safe

- making information and advice clearer, simpler and readily accessible
- involving all stakeholders and developing close working relationships with them
- providing support free from the fear of enforcement
- prioritising work – identifying areas that are well controlled from which the HSC and HSE could withdraw
- changing the way the HSC and HSE communicate.

By 2008, the HSE was consulting on a new strategy to help it reset the direction for health and safety, identifying goals in these key areas:

- the need for strong leadership
- building competence
- workforce involvement
- creating healthier, safer workplaces
- customising support for small businesses
- avoiding catastrophes in high hazard industries
- taking account of wider issues affecting health and safety.

A change of government in 2010 led to a fresh look at the impact of health and safety regulation on businesses, with a review of health and safety by Lord Young, followed by a review of regulations that will report in the autumn of 2011.

Corporate governance

The effective management of risks to health, safety and the environment remains essentially the business of employers. Likewise, effective risk management is now seen as a vital ingredient in the codes of good corporate governance and corporate social responsibility that are an increasingly important feature of business life.

The Turnbull Report of 1999 was the result of an investigation by the Institute of Chartered Accountants in England and Wales into the practice of corporate governance, with particular emphasis on internal control and risk management. The Combined Code on Corporate Governance that followed focused on:

- protection of shareholders' investment and company assets (including reputation) through sound systems of control
- initiation of regular reviews of the effectiveness of controls, in particular finance, operations, compliance and risk management
- reviewing the need for an internal audit function, where this does not already exist.

The Code further states that directors should review the systems of control at least annually.

The government decided not to proceed with regulations requiring mandatory reporting. Directors of quoted companies are instead now required under the Companies Act 2006 to provide a 'business review' or voluntary Operating and Financial Review describing key performance indicators and risks to business, including information about the firm's environmental impact and its employees. The Accounting Standards Board has issued a statement about best practice.

So, by focusing on risk management across the whole of a business, the requirements of health and safety and environmental legislation are being integrated into general management practice. Investors, shareholders, regulators and employees are insisting on the effective management of risks, and that health, safety and the environment take their proper place among the risks to be managed. They can no longer be relegated out of the mainstream of business.

This issue is not one confined to the United Kingdom. Recent financial scandals in the United States and the gaping holes in corporate responsibility that they revealed have concentrated minds on risk management. These concerns have become increasingly important across Europe, particularly since the European Commission issued a Green Paper promoting a European framework for corporate social responsibility in 2001. Following this, in 2004 the European Agency for Safety and Health at Work published a research report, 'Corporate social responsibility and safety and health at work'. It contains 11 case studies showing how enterprises have integrated occupational safety and health issues into corporate social responsibility.

In these ways SHE (safety, health and environment) has come of age. Now recognised as an essential component in the management of a business, the topic is of real interest to directors, shareholders and investors, who are becoming involved in ethical investing and are paying attention to statistics such as those provided by the HSE's performance indices.

Action

Directors therefore have a legal duty to satisfy themselves that proper measures to ensure health, safety and environmental protection are being taken by the company in which they serve (see the Institute of Directors and HSE's free leaflet, *Leading health and safety at work* (INDG417)). In order to fulfil that responsibility, directors should satisfy themselves that:

- the company is at least complying with minimum standards
- the company is going further than mere compliance and creating a culture of safety and the protection of health and the environment sufficient to preserve the reputation of the business, to meet the expectations of

shareholders, customers, employees and the general public, and to ensure that the proper duties of the directors are wholly fulfilled.

References and further reading

This chapter is a summary presentation of the general responsibilities of directors under health and safety law. The HSE website (www.hse.gov.uk) gives access to a very considerable body of more detailed published advice and guidance to assist employers in meeting the specifics of their health and safety responsibilities. The Environment Agency's website (www.environment-agency.gov.uk) provides access to a comprehensive range of information and guidance on a variety of environmental topics (see also Chapter 13). Particular issues can usually be resolved by reference to these websites and many companies will have specialist staff to deal with the detail. Other references may be found in:

Accounting Standards Board. *Reporting Statement: Operating and Financial Review* (ASB Publications, London, 2006) – available online at www.frc.org.uk/images/uploaded/documents/Reporting%20Statements%20OFR%20web.pdf

Business in the Community. *Corporate responsibility index 2002* (BITC Publications, London, 2002)

Companies Act 2006, Ch 46 (HMSO, London)

Department of the Environment, Transport and the Regions. *Revitalising health and safety strategy statement* (HMSO, Norwich, 2000)

Directorate-General for Employment and Social Affairs. *Promoting a European framework for corporate social responsibility*, Green Paper (European Commission, Brussels, 2001)

Edwards v National Coal Board 1949, 1 KB 704

European Agency for Safety and Health at Work. *Corporate social responsibility and health and safety at work*, Research Issue 210 (Office for Official Publications of the European Communities, Luxembourg, 2004)

Health and Safety at Work etc Act 1974, Ch 37 (HMSO, London)

HSC. *A strategy for workplace health and safety in Great Britain to 2010 and beyond* (HSE Books, Sudbury, 2004)

HSE. Corporate Health and Safety Performance Index (CHaSPI), www.chaspi.info-exchange.com (2005)

HSE. Health and Safety Performance Indicator (HSPI) for small and medium-sized enterprises, www.hspi.info-exchange.com (2005)

HSE. *Securing health together. A long-term occupational health strategy for England, Scotland and Wales* (HSE Books, Sudbury, 2000)

HSE. 'The health and safety of Great Britain: Be part of the solution', www.hse.gov.uk/strategy

HSE and the Institute of Directors, free leaflet. *Leading health and safety at work*, INDG417, (HSE Books, Sudbury, 2007)

Institution of Occupational Safety and Health, free document. *Business risk management - getting health and safety firmly on the agenda* (IOSH, Leicester, 2008)

Institution of Occupational Safety and Health, free document. *Making a difference – a basic guide to environmental management for OSH practitioners* (IOSH, Leicester, 2009)

Institution of Occupational Safety and Health, free document. *Promoting a positive culture - a guide to health and safety culture* (IOSH, Leicester, 2004)

Institution of Occupational Safety and Health, free document. *Reporting performance - guidance on including health and safety performance in annual reports* (IOSH, Leicester, 2008)

Institution of Occupational Safety and Health, free document. *Systems in focus – guidance on OSH management systems* (IOSH, Leicester, 2009)

Management of Health and Safety at Work Regulations 1999, SI 1999/3242 (HMSO, London)

Lord Robens. *Safety and health at work: Report of the Committee 1970–72*, CMND 5034 (HMSO, London, 1972)

Turnbull, N. *Internal control: guidance for directors on the Combined Code* (Institute of Chartered Accountants in England and Wales, London, 1999)

Chapter 2
If you get it wrong…

"The law seems like a sort of maze through which a client must be led to safety, a collection of reefs, rocks and underwater hazards through which he or she must be piloted." Sir John Mortimer

The plain fact is that it is an offence to fail to observe any of the duties described in Chapter 1 and, depending on circumstances, the penalties can be swingeing. Of course, no directors worth their salt would act only out of fear of legal consequences, but it is as well to be clear as to what the law demands.

Health and safety offences are set out in detail in Section 33 of the 1974 Act. For directors, Section 37 of the Act is particularly important because it deals with offences by bodies corporate. Where an offence is proved to have been committed with the consent or connivance of, or to have been attributable to any neglect on the part of, any director, manager, secretary or similar officer of the body corporate, they too shall be 'guilty of that offence and liable to be proceeded against and punished accordingly'.

That is no idle threat – as a demolition firm and two of its directors discovered when, in 2004, they were fined a total of £245,000 at Birmingham Crown Court after workers had been exposed to asbestos dust. Also in 2004, the director of a haulage firm was given a seven-year jail sentence for manslaughter following a work-related road crash in which three people died. The company was also fined £50,000. In 2005, a record fine of £15 million was imposed on a gas distribution company in Scotland after an explosion caused by a leaking gas main killed four people in their home.

Penalties for breaching the law protecting the environment are at least as tough. Fines for environmental offences such as fly-tipping, illegal waste operations, packaging contraventions and polluting watercourses are commonly in five figures. A fine of £4 million, later reduced on appeal, was imposed for a serious environmental pollution incident at Milford Haven.

Nor is the tariff getting cheaper. The government, Parliament and the courts are increasingly concerned to toughen the penalties and to place responsibility personally on the shoulders of company directors for breaches of health and safety or environmental law. This is a tendency that is likely to intensify.

Health and safety laws, and laws protecting the environment, are part of the criminal law, not the civil or administrative branches as is sometimes mistakenly believed. There are over 1,000 health and safety prosecutions a year in British courts; these mostly involve corporations, but every year some individuals are also prosecuted. Prosecutions for environmental offences are at a similar level. Most prosecutions of companies result in convictions and fines, some recently running into seven figures. However, individual directors have also been fined and sometimes jailed. Directors have also been disqualified and there is a growing clamour to increase the incidence of holding individuals to personal account for breaches of safety, health and environmental legislation.

The courts

The great majority of the prosecutions take place in the Magistrates' Courts in England and Wales, and the Sheriff Courts in Scotland. In these courts the maximum penalty for most health and safety offences is £20,000, or up to six months' imprisonment.

However, more serious cases may be sent to the Crown Courts, where unlimited fines can be imposed. A civil engineering company was fined £1.2 million in 1999 after a tunnel it was building collapsed under Heathrow Airport. In 2004 a major DIY retailer was fined £550,000 at Birmingham Crown Court after a visitor was crushed against racking by a forklift truck in a store.

Sentencing policy

Most offences are 'triable either way', that is to say that either the prosecutor or the defendant may elect for trial by jury in the higher Crown Courts. Where this is the case, magistrates are advised to consider whether their limited sentencing powers are appropriate. As a result, there is a trend for more health and safety cases to be committed by the magistrates to the higher courts where the penalties imposed can be much more severe, and can include unlimited fines and custodial sentences of up to two years. In early 2007, a large steel company was fined £1.3 million with costs of £1.7 million after three workers were killed in a blast furnace explosion.

Assuming, however, that magistrates hear the case and then decide to convict, after weighing up the seriousness of the offence they will consider the level of penalty. This is usually a fine up to a maximum of £20,000, but may be a custodial sentence of up to six months. While the ability to pay a fine will always be a factor in deciding the penalty, there are other criteria which will be taken into account.

In the case of *R v Howe and Sons (Engineering) Ltd* the Court of Appeal gave guidance on health and safety sentencing, saying that a fine needs to be large enough to bring home to those who manage a company, and to its shareholders, the need to protect the health and safety of workers and the public.

The main points of this landmark case are that:

- fines on companies need to be large enough to make an impact on shareholders
- a company is presumed to be able to pay any fine the court is minded to impose unless information to the contrary is available before the hearing
- a deliberate breach of the legislation by a company or an individual with a view to profit seriously aggravates the offence.

Another recent landmark case, *R v Friskies Petcare UK Ltd*, resulted in guidelines being set out for prosecutors, defendants and the sentencing court in the event of a guilty plea. The guidelines recommended that the salient facts of the case, together with aggravating and mitigating factors, should be presented to the court in the form of schedules, which if possible should be agreed by the parties in advance. There will therefore be no doubt about the basis on which sentence is passed and a higher court dealing with any appeal against the sentence will have the relevant facts. As a result of that case, the Magistrates' Courts should now take into account 'aggravating and mitigating factors' before deciding sentence.

Aggravating factors include:

- a deliberate or reckless breach of the law rather than carelessness
- action or lack of action prompted by financial motives – profit or cost saving
- disregarding warnings from a regulatory authority or the workforce
- awareness of the specific risks likely to arise from action taken
- lack of co-operation with a regulatory authority
- serious extent of damage resulting from the offence (but lack of damage does not render the offence merely technical; it is still serious if there is risk)
- previous offences of a serious nature
- death, serious injury or ill health of humans as consequences of the offence
- damage to animal health or flora
- the need for an expensive clean-up operation
- the defendant carrying out operations without an appropriate licence
- interfering with other lawful activities.

Mitigating factors include:

- prompt admission of responsibility
- timely guilty plea
- steps taken promptly to put matters right
- generally good previous record of health and safety performance
- isolated lapse
- genuine lack of awareness or understanding of specific regulations
- ready co-operation with regulatory authority
- minor role with little personal responsibility.

Guidance on the fining of companies for environmental and health and safety offences has been issued to magistrates through the 'Magistrates' Court sentencing guidelines' by the Magistrates' Association, with the support of the Lord Chancellor and the Lord Chief Justice.

In assessing appropriate penalties for a company, magistrates are advised to look at turnover, profitability and liquidity. If a company does not produce its accounts, the court can assume that the company can pay whatever fine the court imposes. They have other sentencing options:

- discharge, though this will rarely be appropriate
- compensation, which should be considered if there is a specific victim
- directors and senior managers may be summoned before the courts and custodial sentences are available in specific circumstances
- directors may be disqualified under the Company Directors Disqualification Act 1986.

The court may also order the cause of an offence to be remedied, forfeited or destroyed (Section 42 of the 1974 Act).

Manslaughter and 'corporate killing'

In the UK there is a strong groundswell of opinion created by victim support groups, trade unions and lawyers in favour of tougher penalties for causing deaths at work. There is a high risk of prosecution for manslaughter where gross negligence is evident. When four young people were drowned in Lyme Bay in 1999, in an incident in which their canoes capsized in mounting seas, the managing director of the company running the activity centre that organised their expedition was convicted of manslaughter and jailed.

In 2004 the managing director of a heating and ventilation firm was jailed for 12 months for the manslaughter of a 21-year-old apprentice. The young man was burnt to death in a boatyard while cleaning a storage tank, using a highly flammable liquid about which he had not been warned.

While convictions have been secured against individuals blamed for causing deaths at work, there has been considerable debate about the adequacy of the law in dealing with corporate manslaughter. So far there have been several attempts to secure convictions, all of which have failed. For example, a case was taken after the capsize of the *Herald of Free Enterprise* car ferry claimed 188 lives off Zeebrugge in 1987. This case failed because 'the various acts of negligence could not be aggregated and attributed to any individual who was a directing mind' (*R v P&O Ferries (Dover) Ltd*).

The notion of connecting a directing or controlling mind to the act of negligence causing death is important. More recently, following the Southall rail collision in 1997 which resulted in seven deaths and 151 injuries, a judge ruled that a charge of manslaughter against the train company could not succeed because of the need to 'identify some person whose gross negligence was that of

Great Western Trains itself'. In 2004 a judge threw out manslaughter cases which had been attempted against Railtrack following the Hatfield train derailment, an action which rekindled arguments about the need for reform.

In 1996 the Law Commission had recommended changes in the law that would have the effect of enabling prosecutors to secure the conviction of companies for the offence of 'corporate killing'. After a decade of consultation, the Corporate Manslaughter and Corporate Homicide Bill finally passed into law.

The Corporate Manslaughter and Corporate Homicide Act 2007

The Corporate Manslaughter and Corporate Homicide Act 2007 (CMCHA) came into effect on 6 April 2008, covering England, Wales, Scotland and Northern Ireland. The Act creates a new corporate offence: in future an organisation may be found guilty of corporate manslaughter (corporate homicide in Scotland) if death is caused by a gross breach of its relevant duty of care that is substantially due to the way in which its activities are managed or organised by senior management.

Senior managers are those who play a significant role in the decision-making or management of the organisation. The relevant duty of care is effectively any duty owed under the law of negligence and includes duties owed by an organisation to its employees and others working for it, such as contractors; duties owed by occupiers of premises to visitors; and duties owed in connection with various business activities such as construction, maintenance, supply of goods or services and any other activity carried out for commercial purposes. Organisations include corporations, partnerships, trade unions, employers' bodies, police forces and certain government bodies.

While a conviction under the new Act may lead to an unlimited fine it does not itself incur a penalty of imprisonment. Nevertheless, individual directors and senior managers must bear in mind that they may still be prosecuted as individuals either for gross negligence manslaughter and/or a breach of Section 37 of the HSWA. The maximum penalty for gross negligence manslaughter is life imprisonment.

The two Acts are closely associated, being based on the duty of care. Investigations by the authorities are also likely to be closely associated. The police will investigate deaths with the technical support of the HSE, both authorities already being bound by the principles contained in *Work-related deaths: a protocol for liaison*. With the consent of the Director of Public Prosecutions where the public interest and evidential tests are satisfied, the Crown Prosecution Service will prosecute. Cases under CMCHA are 'indictable only' and will therefore be tried in the Crown Court in front of a judge and jury.

The consequences are likely to be severe where prosecutions succeed. Fines are unlimited and in 2010 new guidelines for offences under the Corporate Manslaughter and Corporate Homicide Act 2007 and the Health and Safety at Work etc Act 1974 were issued by the Sentencing Guidelines Council which mean corporations now face very heavy penalties for breaches of their duty of care towards employees.

Courts also have the power under the CMCHA to make remedial orders and 'publicity orders'. Aside from the potentially very high fines that could ensue if they are convicted of the new offence after a death at work, corporations will be concerned about bad publicity and damage to reputation and brand. But as the new Act does not impose any new health and safety duties on organisations beyond those that already exist under the HSWA, an organisation that is already meeting its duties under the 1974 Act should have little to fear.

The Health and Safety (Offences) Act 2008

This Act, which unusually began life as a Private Member's Bill, has increased the range of offences subject to the maximum fine of £20,000 in the Magistrates' Courts and has made custodial sentences an option for more offences. But the most serious offences will still be triable in the Crown Courts and can thus be subject to heavier sentencing.

Directors may also be disqualified at the court's discretion: for up to five years in the lower courts and up to 15 years in the higher.

How should directors respond?

So how should directors and senior managers behave in the face of these duties and dire consequences of failure? In spite of the legal arguments described, it still looks pretty daunting. Clearly, a company labelled as a corporate killer would suffer major damage to its reputation and goodwill. Directors seen to fail in their duty would be subject not only to the law but to the judgment of shareholders and often of the press. The extent of such responsibility and exposure has led many to wonder whether they should shoulder the liabilities of a company director, particularly in a non-executive capacity.

However, there is some real help from official sources that shows how, by appropriate action, such directors can properly carry out their responsibilities and protect themselves from liability.

Key principles

In 2007, in response to calls for a change in the law concerning directors' health and safety duties, the HSC and the Institute of Directors collaborated in producing a free guidance leaflet entitled *Leading health and safety at work*.

Their advice is based on the essential principles of:

- strong and active leadership from the top
  - visible, active commitment from the board
  - establishing effective 'downward' communication systems and management structures
  - integration of good health and safety management with business decisions
- worker involvement
  - engaging the workforce in the promotion and achievement of safe and healthy conditions
  - effective 'upward' communication
  - providing high-quality training
- assessment and review
  - identifying and managing health and safety risks
  - accessing (and following) competent advice
  - monitoring, reviewing and reporting progress.

Action

These recommendations are discussed in more detail in following chapters. However, as a minimum, directors should satisfy themselves that:

- they are all giving health and safety and environmental leadership
- they know what their employees think of the company's health, safety and environmental performance
- they are involving the workforce properly
- the board is sufficiently aware of risks to health and safety and the environment in the company

- the board really knows how the company is performing
- there is a director who is officially and effectively the safety, health and environment champion

References and further reading

HSE and the Institute of Directors, free leaflet. *Leading health and safety at work*, INDG417, (HSE Books, Sudbury, 2007)

Magistrates' Association sentencing guidelines (www.sentencing-guidelines.gov.uk /guidelines/other/magistrates.html)

Ministry of Justice website, www.justice.gov.uk/guidance/manslaughter

R v Friskies Petcare UK Ltd 2000, 2 Cr App R (S) 401

R v Howe and Sons (Engineers) Ltd 1999, 2 All ER 249

Turnbull, N. *Internal control: guidance for directors on the Combined Code* (Institute of Chartered Accountants in England and Wales, London, 1999)

Chapter 3
The enforcers

"The appropriate use of enforcement powers, including prosecution, is important, both to secure compliance with the law and to ensure that those who have duties under it may be held to account for failures to safeguard health, safety and welfare." Health and Safety Executive's Enforcement Policy Statement, 2009

The government has urged the authorities and the courts to get tough with companies and individuals who wilfully flout the law. These are not idle threats. In recent years several directors have been sent to jail and others have been disqualified under the Company Directors Disqualification Act 1986. It is therefore important to understand how enforcement operates.

The job is shared between the HSE and the 400 or so local authorities. Local authorities and the Environment Agency are responsible for enforcing laws protecting the environment, which are discussed in more detail in Chapter 13.

The HSE has a duty to make adequate arrangements for enforcement of health and safety law. It appoints inspectors to do the enforcement but also carries out many other functions, such as conducting and disseminating the results of research and providing information and advice. Over the years, it has published voluminous general and technical guidance, much of which is now available online (www.hse.gov.uk) or from HSE Books (PO Box 1999, Sudbury, Suffolk CO10 2WA).

Enforcement policy
The HSC has enunciated five key principles in its 'Enforcement policy statement' to which the enforcing authorities are urged to conform:

- consistency
- proportionality
- targeting
- transparency
- accountability.

This means that in practice inspectors will try to apply the same approach to enforcement in similar circumstances, wherever they are found. They will try to match the enforcement action to the seriousness of the failure to comply, target the more serious risks and the worse performing companies, be open about their decision-making and be accountable for the actions they take. The full text of the policy statement can be found on the HSE website.

The Hampton Review

The HSE's intended approach to inspection is risk-based as well as proportionate, trying to ensure that its costly inspection resources are aimed where significant risks to the health and safety of workers or the public exist or at companies whose track record in managing risks is poor.

In the 2004 Budget the Chancellor of the Exchequer asked Sir Philip Hampton to report on what could be done to reduce the administrative burden of regulation on business. The Hampton Review looked at how to cut the time spent by businesses on form-filling and responding to inspections from numerous regulatory bodies while making sure that they still complied with regulations. In March 2005 his review recommended:

- the use of risk-based inspection, which should ensure those more likely to breach regulations are caught
- tougher penalties to clamp down on the most persistent offenders
- setting targets for reductions in form-filling for business
- merging 31 smaller regulatory bodies into seven larger bodies that are better able to develop and operate risk-based inspection and ensure that inspections are 'joined up'.

The HSE and the Environment Agency, two of the larger regulatory bodies, remain. Their approach to enforcement was generally endorsed by the review.

Powers of inspectors

It helps to understand how inspectors generally behave. Formally appointed by the enforcing authorities, they are given considerable statutory powers. They may enter premises at any reasonable time for enforcement purposes or at any time if in their opinion the situation may be dangerous.

Inspectors may take a police officer with them if they anticipate serious obstruction. They may also take other authorised people, examine and investigate whatever is judged necessary, direct things to be left undisturbed or take possession of them for examination, take measurements, photographs or recordings, and take samples and have them tested. They can require the production and copying of documents and can request other facilities and assistance.

Inspectors have the important right to ask questions of any individuals if they believe they are able to give relevant information, and to require them to sign a declaration of the truth of the answers. The person being interviewed may nominate someone else to be present; otherwise the only other people present will be those authorised by the inspector.

Inspectors will follow the approach to enforcement laid down by Parliament in the Regulatory Enforcement and Sanctions Act 2008. They are generally well trained, very professional and have a deserved reputation for fairness. They are obliged to tell you the name and address of their line manager if you wish to complain about their actions. They should carry their warrant, which they can be asked to produce if an employer is in doubt about their status. They can also be expected to offer a business card containing their individual details.

The responsible employer who genuinely wishes to improve health and safety performance and who respects the role of the inspector should have little to fear from them. Inspectors see their enforcement role as including an advisory function and they will generally indicate what needs to be done, and give time to do it, before wielding the big stick. Nonetheless, there are many occasions when perfectly reasonable people feel that they have been put upon and are angered at what they consider a heavy-handed implementation of the law.

This arises partly from the way that the legislation is drafted. It is, as we have said, intended not to be prescriptive, giving detailed requirements to fit every eventuality. Instead, it sets out general principles and modes of risk assessment and expects employers to look to the best way to carry through those responsibilities. The law therefore envisages that the response will be different in different circumstances. It is the end result that matters, not the means of achieving it.

When inspectors come into the picture and proffer advice, it is in that context. Their experience and knowledge can be of great help and should not lightly be ignored. Yet, the employer is the responsible person under the Act. He or she has general as well as specific duties and has every right to discover whether the advice proffered is based closely on the statutory provision or whether it is the inspector's own judgment. If the latter, then the director responsible is at liberty to choose another way of meeting the desired end.

The legislation specifically gives such flexibility and its proper use can overcome the problems that can arise when a new inspector appears to want a different solution from his or her predecessor. Thus, an inspector who insists that there is only one way of ensuring that a kitchen floor will meet food hygiene requirements is claiming prescription where none exists. However, one who demands that staff lavatories are marked so that they indicate which sex can use them is legally correct, but he or she should not go on to specify how.

If, therefore, a particular solution recommended by an inspector seems expensive or burdensome and an alternative properly meets the case, it is entirely reasonable to question the legal base of the inspector's advice and the reasons why he or she preferred that solution. It is then up to the responsible director to decide what to do. Clearly, it would be foolish not to take the inspector seriously. It would be particularly so where there is an established, well-researched solution to making a particular process or machine safe. Where such a standard of good practice exists, an inspector should accept that meeting it achieves compliance with the legal duty to ensure health and safety 'so far as is reasonably practicable'.

Nonetheless, inspectors should not make prescriptive what the law makes flexible. 'SHE awareness' is not meant to be a series of rules but a culture within which a business learns to work in a safe, healthy and environmentally friendly way. We would be foolish not to learn from the experience of others but, in the end, we have to make the culture our own. It is this which the law seeks to ensure.

Prosecutions

That attitude does not, of course, constitute an excuse to avoid responsibility. Indeed, it places the responsibility squarely on the shoulders of the directors. Sometimes they fail so clearly in their duty that they find themselves in court.

Inspectors are well aware of the guidelines followed by the courts and will take them into account when recommending cases for prosecution.

The HSE's inspectors are empowered to prosecute cases themselves in the Magistrates' Courts in England and Wales and often do so, but not in the higher courts. However, it is not uncommon now for them to use solicitor advocates or to brief counsel for cases which are likely to be defended. Solicitors generally prosecute cases for local authorities. In Scotland cases are pursued by the Procurator Fiscal.

The more serious offences are likely to be tried in the Crown Courts. Cases are not usually referred to the Crown Prosecution Service (CPS) unless there is evidence to support a possible charge of manslaughter, in which case an investigation involving the police will have first taken place.

Improvement and prohibition notices

The 1974 Act gave inspectors new powers to serve notices. The expectation that these would become the principal enforcement tool has proved right: several thousand notices are served each year, whereas the number of prosecutions is around a thousand.

Where inspectors find situations that in their opinion are in serious breach of the law they may serve an 'improvement notice'. This sets out what is wrong and specifies a time by which it must be remedied. If they think there is danger likely to cause injury or death they may decide to stop the job immediately by serving a 'prohibition notice'. Failure to comply with a notice is regarded as a serious offence. There are rights of appeal to employment tribunals.

For some years now the HSE has been 'naming and shaming' offenders by publishing details of convictions and notices on its website, www.hse.gov.uk. The Environment Agency also publishes a report on the best and worst performers of the year.

Action

Directors will want to satisfy themselves that:

- they know whether their company has any convictions for health and safety offences
- they know the record of their suppliers and contractors, particularly those who work on the company's own sites
- they are informed of any enforcement notices served on the company; what remedial action has been taken; and whether lessons have been learned
- they have assessed the attitude of the enforcing authorities towards the company
- they are in full compliance with the law.

References and further reading

Health and Safety at Work etc Act 1974, Ch 37 (HMSO, London)

HSC. *Enforcement policy statement*, HSC15 (HSE Books, Sudbury, 2002)

HSE website index: www.hse.gov.uk/index.htm

HSE and the Institute of Directors, free leaflet. *Leading health and safety at work*, INDG417, (HSE Books, Sudbury, 2007)

Magistrates' Association sentencing guidelines (www.sentencing-guidelines.gov.uk /guidelines/other/magistrates.html)

Management of Health and Safety at Work Regulations 1999, SI 1999/3242 (HMSO, London)

Regulatory Enforcement and Sanctions Act 2008

Chapter 4
Accidents and ill health – avoidable risks to the business

"Accidents will occur in the best regulated families…" Mr Micawber in 'David Copperfield' by Charles Dickens

Most of us in business have had our whinge about health and safety and the increasing cost of environmental protection. There are some lurid anecdotes about over-zealous health and safety officers, piffling rules and ludicrous regulation. Some columnists make their living bringing these to our attention, often in highly colourful ways. It is also a particular habit of the British to suggest, almost entirely incorrectly, that most of these examples stem from bossy decisions made in Brussels by unelected bureaucrats.

It is no part of this book's purpose to excuse those occasions when regulation and enforcement are seen to be asinine, over-costly and over the top. Nonetheless, a word of warning does seem appropriate. Newspapers rarely make a story out of regulations that save lives or inspectors and advisers who help to protect health and the environment from serious damage. Nor is it often mentioned that almost all the regulations that have a bearing on safety, health and environment are based on UK legislation and practice. Indeed, the UK has in many ways become the leader in these fields in the European Union, and our example is increasingly followed on the continent.

It is also a salutary lesson for all of us to face the real costs of accidents – even with the regulatory framework about which we so often complain. In recent years there have been many highly publicised and highly charged major incidents in the UK and abroad, such as the explosion at Flixborough, the capsize of the *Herald of Free Enterprise*, the fire on the Piper Alpha oil platform, the collapse of the Fréjus dam, the Space Shuttle disasters, the explosion of the nuclear reactor at Chernobyl, the toxic gas escapes at Seveso and Bhopal, the sinking of the *Exxon Valdez*, the Abbeystead explosion, the train crashes at Southall, Paddington and

Hatfield and the major incidents at Toulouse, Texas City, Buncefield and the Gulf of Mexico. Some of these have destroyed the reputations or even the very existence of the organisations responsible.

These are the horrible accidents that come to everyone's mind because they have been splashed across the pages of our newspapers and featured again and again on our news broadcasts. Yet for every one of these, there are a thousand lesser incidents that have not hit the headlines but which have cost significant sums, ruined health and lives and damaged the environment. Many of these lesser incidents have cost directors and their companies dear. That is why we have to ask ourselves a couple of simple questions: 'Have we thought about the effect that such an event, occurring in the context of our company's business, could have? Could our company even survive such an event?'

Even when accidents are not as serious as this, the negative effects on a business from an incident or series of incidents can add up to a very considerable commercial risk. What is particularly true is that the costs that most companies see and measure are often merely the tip of a very large iceberg. Like the officers of the *Titanic*, we ignore them at our peril.

There are the very substantial hidden costs such as wasted managerial time, loss of key staff, contractual delivery delays, loss of contracts, low morale, high staff turnover, replacement training costs, and increased insurance premiums. The list can go on and on. This is quite apart from the damage that may occur to brand and reputation, which may be the most serious blow to the assets in the business.

In the UK there are, on average, two fatal accidents at work every three days, not including work-related traffic accidents. Almost every one could have been prevented had the health and safety management not been so weak. Even in non-fatal accidents, many people suffer serious injury or permanent damage to their health. Indeed, every year some 25,000 people leave the workforce, never to return, because of harm they have suffered at work.

The HSE estimated that accidents and ill health at work in Great Britain in 2001/02 had cost employers between £3.9 billion and £7.8 billion, employees between £10.1 billion and £14.7 billion, the economy between £13.1 billion and £22.2 billion and society as a whole between £20 billion and £31.8 billion. By 2008, the HSE had raised its estimate of the overall cost to £36 billion.

These figures are the effect of the loss of output, business interruption, cost of medical treatment, administration and compensation, insurance payments and property damage. This equates to the staggering figure of between 5 and 10 per cent of the trading profits of all UK industrial companies put together. That's something between £200 and £400 for every employee, every year.

None of this is an excuse for unnecessary interference, badly thought-out regulation or heavy-handed enforcement. It is, however, a proper justification for a sensible regime to protect the health, safety and environment of people at work.

And it is at the company level that losses from poor health, safety and environmental management really come home to roost. Many firms are blissfully unaware of the true costs of the simplest visit to a first aider. If, in total, accidents at work equate to around 10 per cent of trading profits across industry, the companies with the worst records are paying out huge sums, almost wholly avoidably. Individual companies such as South West Water have conducted their own research and, taken with the results of the HSE's inquiries, the findings are quite startling. Even in small companies employing no more than 100 people, the costs of accidents can easily equate to £40,000 a year. Most companies have little or no idea about what these accidents and ill health cost them and, if they measure it all, they usually consider only the direct costs. They choose to ignore, or are simply unaware of, the indirect costs, which are often considerably greater. The HSE has published a series of case studies showing, for example, that effective health and safety management saved one company £12 for every £1 it spent.

Health and safety can, in that sense, be regarded as a profit centre. Reducing incidents and ill health can have a direct effect on the bottom line. To be even more direct, if you think improving health and safety is a low priority for your business, or just too expensive, think what it would be like to cope with a serious accident.

The good news is that studies published in the past by the HSE have shown that 70 per cent of incidents at work are preventable by good management. Some leading companies go much further and regard all incidents, including 'near misses' (ie incidents that did not result in an accident through good luck, but clearly could have done), as preventable. Examination of root causes during

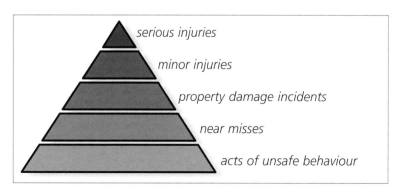

The total loss triangle

investigation bears out this view. Companies following a 'total loss' approach learn from the experience they gain in investigation and take steps to ensure that similar problems cannot recur. This is a positive way of bringing risks and costs under control when things have gone wrong.

However, many companies still suffer from a negative culture that focuses on attaching the blame and passing the buck rather than accepting responsibility, learning, and taking steps to control the risks identified by any investigation.

Proper use of the 'RIDDOR' (Reporting of Injuries, Diseases and Dangerous Occurrences Regulations) requirements is often an aid to changing the blame culture. In any case, your company must report certain incidents, such as accidents resulting in more than three days off work and cases of work-related ill health, to the enforcing authority, which may decide to investigate. If that requirement is treated as part of a process that automatically looks at accidents and seeks to discover their underlying causes and take remedial action, RIDDOR can become a valuable tool rather than an encumbrance.

In fact, the HSE investigates fewer than 20 per cent of these major injury events, but when it does, the incident may well lead to prosecution, as the evidence uncovered often discloses a breach of the law. Invariably in the case of a fatality its investigations will go right to the top of the company's management structure and examine directors' personal responsibility. In other cases, your insurance company may want to investigate, and, of course, there could be a civil claim for compensation.

There are about 100,000 successful personal injury claims in the UK every year. Some firms of solicitors are offering 'no win, no fee' services to sue companies for accidents at work and ill health arising from workplace conditions. The TUC calculates that trade unions win over £300 million in compensation for their members every year. In many cases, the cost and reputational damage involved in defending such actions mean that companies pay up, even where a case might not be won if it came to court. Accident prevention is, therefore, the only sure defence.

Good practice is the first step in ensuring a good health, safety and environmental record. However, it is important to investigate why things go wrong as an effective way to prevent repetition, and directors can do much to ensure that there is a culture that encourages this. Too often, minor incidents occur that could have been avoided.

That is why, in 2001, the HSC consulted on a proposed explicit duty on companies to investigate their own accidents. While that proposal is not being carried forward into law for the time being, it is obviously good practice for companies to instigate a system that ensures that all dangerous incidents are investigated, whether they have actually caused injury or not. There is currently an implicit duty to investigate such incidents, with an explicit requirement to do so only in certain circumstances (such as those governed by the COMAH Regulations). This will often reveal the root cause of problems and enable management to find solutions (see also Chapter 10, Monitoring).

Setting out to cut costs by preventing expensive incidents is a positive step, will motivate managers to do better, and can be measured. Understanding the true costs of a company's accidents and ill health events and collecting costs data on a systematic basis allow the company to establish a financial baseline against which the effectiveness of preventative measures can be judged.

Action

Directors should therefore ensure that:

- there is a strategy for controlling losses occurring from accidents and ill health
- the board is told about any incidents that occur in the company
- the risk manager provides information about company performance in preventing injuries and ill health. What are such incidents costing the company? What about 'near misses'?
- if this information does not exist, it is collected, analysed and presented to the board, with recommendations for improving control, by a specified date. It is important that the report is put on the board's agenda for discussion and action, not simply 'below the line'
- the board knows what your safety representatives think and directors have the opportunity to talk to them, particularly on site visits. Get the board to decide what to do about the recommended actions and ask for a progress report by a specified date. Be prepared to nag until you are satisfied. Don't feel satisfied until you are confident about assurances. You may have to explain yourself in court one day.

References and further reading

Bird, F E. *Management guide to loss control* (Institute Press, Atlanta, Georgia, 1974)

Gwyther, R. *The Frank Davies Project: health protection and accident prevention as business imperatives in the water industry* (South West Water, 2000)

HSE. *Reduce risks, cut costs*, INDG355 (HSE Books, Sudbury. 2002)

HSE. *Business benefits of health and safety* (www.hse.gov.uk/businessbenefits)

HSE. *Good health is good business – employers' guide*, MISC130 (HSE Books, Sudbury, 1999)

HSE. *Annual costs: Work out yours. Annual accident calculator and incident costs calculator* (www.hse.gov.uk/costs/accidentcost_calc/accident_costs_intro.asp, 2005)

HSE. *Interim update of the 'Costs to Britain of workplace accidents and work-related ill health'* (www.hse.gov.uk/statistics/pdf/costs.pdf, 2004)

HSE. *The costs of accidents at work*, HSG96 (HSE Books, Sudbury, 1997)

HSE. *The costs to the British economy of work accidents and work-related ill health*, HSG101, second edition (HSE Books, Sudbury, 1999)

Reporting of Injuries, Diseases and Dangerous Occurrences Regulations 1995, SI 1995/3163 (HMSO, London)

Chapter 5
Risk assessment

"A damned close-run thing," said the Duke of Wellington, after the Battle of Waterloo. He had held Napoleon's army at bay all day, calculating that the battle could be won when the Prussians arrived to reinforce the British and Allied forces. The Prussians were late in reaching the battlefield, but Wellington's assessment was correct, and a famous victory was won.

Good soldiers and business people know that accurate risk assessment is an essential part of risk management. Risk assessment enables you to set priorities, allocate resources and take the right kind of action to ensure the protection and success of the enterprise.

Failure to get risk assessment right means that risks cannot be appropriately managed and that is always wasteful of resources. It can sometimes be catastrophic. A fire and explosion at the Piper Alpha offshore oil installation in 1988 killed 167 people, the installation was destroyed and the operating company left the North Sea. Fires and explosions at a Milford Haven oil refinery in 1994 knocked out 10 per cent of UK refining capability for several months and resulted in a hefty fine for breach of health and safety law.

For any business, the loss of key workers or plant in an accident is likely to damage the company's capability to satisfy its customers. But it is not simply about safety. Failure to recognise health risks and take sufficient care of employees at risk can also result in long-term harm both to workers and companies, as in the case of asbestos exposure and the deaths and major compensation claims which have followed.

Avoiding these consequences through prevention has to be the wiser course. The only question is 'how do we know?' There is no sense in hiding one's head in the sand. A court does not take ignorance as a defence. It asks: 'Could and should the management have known?' That makes risk assessment an essential technique, not only to avoid damage to the company but to protect a director against blame. It identifies hazards, acknowledges the existence and severity of risks, and helps to select the right control measures and prioritise action. This allows risks at work to be properly managed and brought to acceptable levels.

The law on assessing risks

Life is full of risks and, in order to survive, the human race has had to learn to avoid the worst of them and learn lessons at the same time. Away from work we are generally allowed to take chances. Indeed, many of us are irritated when officious people suggest that they know best and protect us against our will. The 'nanny state' is now the scourge of all political parties and it is the stuff of dinner party conversation to complain of some preposterous new invasion of our liberties.

However, when people are employed it is accepted that the employer has a duty of care. People must not be exposed to danger while carrying out their jobs or legitimately visiting business premises. Indeed, in some cases, those who have been illegitimately visiting premises have managed to get compensation for injury although many commentators find this a pretty difficult proposition to accept. Nonetheless, almost everyone would accept that it is right that risk prevention and risk reduction have been made mandatory to protect the health and safety of employees and those who are affected by a business. Increasingly, too, we understand that the environment needs protection from actions that would cause lasting damage, and that individuals and companies must be dissuaded from the careless approach of the past, which has left us with such an expensive clean-up legacy today. However, the immediate effect on individuals of health and safety breaches has meant that health and safety law has been developed further and for longer than the equivalent environmental legislation.

The 1974 Act requires all employers to ensure, so far as is reasonably practicable, the health, safety and welfare at work of all their employees. They must also conduct their undertaking in such a way as to ensure, so far as is reasonably practicable, that others not in their employment who may be affected by the work activity are not exposed to risks to their health and safety.

These requirements clearly imply assessment of risks, but in 1989 the European Union introduced the Framework Directive that made the implication specific. Now, all European enterprises operate on a level playing field, as all are required to ensure the management of risks including the carrying out of risk assessments. The UK version of this law was contained in the Management of Health and Safety at Work Regulations. These came into effect in 1993 together with an approved code of practice explaining risk assessment in some detail. There was a revision in 1999.

In essence the Management Regulations require employers to:

- assess work-related risks, including fire, to employees and other people (there are also special requirements for assessing risks to young people and expectant mothers)
- make effective arrangements for planning, organising, controlling, monitoring and reviewing risk controls
- appoint at least one competent person to help them comply with the law
- give employees information about the risks and the risk controls.

These are the basic rules but there are other more specific health and safety regulations which also require risk assessments to be done. The best known examples of these regulate substances hazardous to health (COSHH), display screen equipment, and manual handling (see the references section at the end of this chapter).

Directors and risk assessment

The subject of health and safety risk assessment may seem complicated and technical and therefore best left to experts. Indeed, the Management Regulations require employers to appoint someone competent to help them with this work and it may be tempting just to leave them to it. But it is vital for directors to understand what is required so that they can judge whether it is being done properly. Poor risk assessment – and failure to implement a good risk assessment – leads to poor management of health and safety and could make the business and the director liable to serious consequences.

The HSC declared that 'we will simplify the concept of risk assessment to make it relevant and available to all and to ensure a sensible approach to risk management. The HSC will make it clear that risk assessment is a simple, relevant and effective tool.' This was a necessary response to a perceived over-reliance on risk assessment as a process, which some believe has led to unnecessary aversion to risks and fuelled the 'compensation culture'.

Hazard and risk

Risk assessment should be kept as simple as possible but it is a subject which has certainly attracted its share of jargon. 'Hazard' and 'risk' are words used a good deal by experts. They may seem to mean the same thing but they are in fact different concepts.

A 'hazard' is something with the potential to cause harm. 'Risk' is the likelihood of that potential being realised combined with the severity of the harm. A hazard could be as simple as a broken bottle lying in a gangway. The risk of someone treading on the broken glass and cutting their foot is fairly high. Removal of the hazard by sweeping up the glass is clearly 'reasonably practicable' and once that is done there is no direct risk of harm occurring. Even so there is general risk that the use of glass bottles may cause a hazard.

An important judgment in the Court of Appeal has helped define what 'risk' means. Essentially it said that the word should be interpreted as conveying the 'idea of a possibility of danger' (*R v Board of Trustees of the Science Museum*).

Most risks can be reduced to an acceptably safe level by taking the right measures. Even something as hazardous as petrol may present an insignificant chance of causing harm if the risk is adequately controlled. After all, millions of cars are filled up on garage forecourts every day by ordinary members of the public without much mishap. This is because of good standards of safety in storage, safe design of pumps, and sensible behaviour.

Employers are expected by law to do what is reasonably practicable to make sure that all risks are minimised in this way. This means that they need to calculate the size of the risk on the one hand, and the sacrifice in money, time or trouble in reducing it on the other. Only if there is gross disproportion between the two, and the risk is insignificant in relation to the sacrifice, does the law allow that it is not reasonably practicable to reduce the risk further. In *R v Chargot Ltd and others*, the House of Lords emphasised that *prima facie* the employer has failed to ensure health and safety where there has been an injury.

Not every risk can be completely eliminated. Often that is acceptable, as the remoteness of the danger and its lack of seriousness mean that it is reasonable for people to live with it. However, at the other end of the scale there are some risks that society deems too great to be acceptable at all and this leads to the prohibition of the circumstances giving rise to the risk. For example, even limited exposure to some carcinogenic substances is regarded as so dangerous that their use has been banned.

In most cases it will generally be reasonably practicable to reduce the risk to an acceptable level even if it cannot be entirely eliminated. Arguments suggesting that it is too difficult to minimise risk are often popular. It is suggested that people should look after themselves and that they have only themselves to blame if they are foolish enough not to be awake to danger. Such attitudes are widespread. But it is noticeable how soon they disappear when a general contention is replaced by a specific accident, when very soon employers find they are blamed. If then they are found to have failed to reduce a risk where it would be reasonably practicable to do so and consequently there is a serious accident, the courts are unlikely to treat them leniently. Indeed, it is as well to accept that we live in a world that wants a scapegoat. Accidents do not just happen: there has to be someone to blame. Even those who eat too much try to blame their obesity on the fast food industry. Now, this may be very hard and indeed it may be damaging to society; the litigiousness that it brings is certainly expensive and restricting. Nevertheless, this attitude is a fact of life and employers need to take it into account when they are looking at the issues. We are not primarily concerned with philosophy but with practical reality and, in the real world, employers get blamed whether it is fair or not.

In recognition of this, the rules apply to all businesses and require employers to carry out 'suitable and sufficient' risk assessments for the purpose of identifying the measures they need to take to comply with health and safety law. 'Suitable and sufficient' is not defined, but common sense indicates that this means the job has to be done properly.

Employers must appoint a 'competent person' to assist them in undertaking measures to comply with the law. The law is not very specific about what 'competence' means; the Management of Health and Safety at Work Regulations 1999 say that a person may be regarded as competent 'where he has sufficient training and experience or knowledge and other qualities to enable him properly to assist in undertaking the measures'.

In practice, employers would be wise to ensure that anyone they appoint in-house is competent to carry out the work, or employ the services of a consultancy with a good record and reputation in this field. If they choose to do the latter, it is often best to go to those who specialise in advising on these areas of corporate responsibility rather than some adjunct of a company whose real expertise is in accountancy or general corporate legal work.

It is important, in any case, to identify whether a company uses machinery or processes for which particular sets of regulations apply and make specific requirements for assessing risks to do, for example, with manual handling, display screen equipment, noise, substances hazardous to health, asbestos, lead, ionising radiation, major hazards and personal protective equipment. It is quite likely that several sets of regulations will apply to different work activities within a business. The regulations share common features but there are some important differences of which your health and safety adviser or consultant should be aware.

Risk assessment

Although it will be the expert who is charged with carrying out or supervising the risk assessment, the director will need to be aware of five essential steps in assessing risks to health and safety if he or she is to be satisfied that all are satisfactorily covered:

- identification of hazards
- identification of people at risk
- assessment of the risks from the hazards identified
- recording and communicating significant findings, including identified controls
- reviewing the assessments.

Identifying hazards

First, all significant hazards need to be identified. This is obviously crucial. It requires the physical examination of workplaces, machinery and plant, activities such as transport operations and working at height, checking storage and use of hazardous substances such as fuels, solvents and gases. Suppliers' data sheets and manuals will provide vital information about substances and the equipment needed to handle them safely. It is good practice to consult the workforce, whether through the appointed safety representatives or more widely, because they will often know most about what is going on, and what is involved in their work. Reference to accident and ill health records can help pinpoint blackspots.

Identifying people at risk

Secondly, the kinds of people at risk need to be identified. Trainees, young or inexperienced workers and pregnant women may be particularly vulnerable. Visitors to your sites, including contractors, cleaners and the like, need to be kept in mind, as well as any members of the public who could be affected by your company's operations. It is important to know where and how they might be harmed, for example by forklift truck movements.

Assessing the risks

Thirdly, the risks from the identified hazards need to be assessed. Existing control measures must be reviewed and if necessary updated or revised. The law requires regular assessment so that more can be done to reduce risks where this is reasonably practicable. Conducting these risk assessments need not involve elaborate or bureaucratic procedures. The aim is to reduce risks as much as reasonably practicable and therefore the key questions are 'how likely is a hazard to cause harm and how bad will it be?'

The answer should help managers to prioritise actions. The risks can then be ranked as high, medium or low, with pointers as to whether any action is needed to reduce or eliminate a risk, and details of the precautions or control measures that will be necessary to comply with the law. During this stage of the process it is important to make sure that the workforce is consulted through its safety representatives or, where there are none, by more general discussion. These consultations will often lead to valuable suggestions for reducing risks.

Sometimes it is possible to get rid of a hazard altogether, for example by substituting a non-flammable solvent in a process for one that presents a risk of fire or explosion. But zero risk is seldom achievable. Even after all precautions have been taken, some risks may well remain. For example, the non-flammable solvent may be toxic. Any such residual risks should also be ranked high, medium or low, so that further action can be prioritised.

This approach is essentially qualitative. More complicated mathematics, sometimes called 'quantified risk assessment' (QRA), may be needed to deal with particular uncertainties. If your business is, say, nuclear power generation or large-scale manufacturing of chemicals, such an approach would be necessary and normal. But for most companies such sophistication will be unnecessary.

Recording significant findings

The fourth step is to record the significant findings of the risk assessment, and to inform your employees. This written record is not in a prescribed form but it will be most useful if it follows the steps of the risk assessment process and identifies the hazards, the people at risk, the level of the risks assessed (high, medium, low) and their control measures. Reference to manufacturers' and suppliers' documentation can be particularly helpful here.

Reviewing

Finally, the law requires the risk assessments to be kept under review. While there are no compulsory intervals between revisions, they should certainly be revised at least whenever significant changes occur which could introduce new risks, or when there is reason to believe they are no longer valid (eg after incidents, complaints or audit failures).

By following this scheme, control measures ranging from changes in systems of work, elimination or substitution of substances (for example, a less toxic chemical being substituted for the one in use) and process containment to engineering controls (for example, guarding of dangerous machinery or extraction of toxic fumes) can sensibly and reasonably be introduced. Sometimes, but only as a last resort, risk assessment will point to management needing to issue and insist on the use of suitable personal protective equipment. All this must be backed up by effective training and supervision and a high standard of welfare facilities.

More information about specific hazards and controls is in Part 2.

> ## Action
> Directors will need to ensure that:
>
> - the company has complete and comprehensive risk assessments
> - those assessments are up to date
> - they know who conducted them and that they were competent to do so
> - employees were consulted
> - they know the whereabouts and security of the documentation
> - the findings have been properly and effectively communicated to workers
> - the risk assessments have been appropriately reviewed in a timely fashion.

References and further reading

Control of Asbestos Regulations 2006, SI 2006/2739 (HMSO, London)

Control of Lead at Work Regulations 2002, SI 2002/2676 (HMSO, London)

Control of Substances Hazardous to Health Regulations 2002, SI 2002/2677 (HMSO, London)

Health and Safety (Display Screen Equipment) Regulations 1992, SI 1992/2792 (HMSO, London)

HSE. *Control of lead at work. Control of Lead at Work Regulations 2002 – Approved Code of Practice and guidance*, L132 (HSE Books, Sudbury, 2002)

HSE. *Control of substances hazardous to health. Control of Substances Hazardous to Health Regulations 2002 – Approved Code of Practice and guidance*, L5 (fourth edition) (HSE Books, Sudbury, 2002)

HSE. *Display screen equipment at work. Health and Safety (Display Screen Equipment) Regulations 1992 – guidance on Regulations*, L26 (HSE Books, Sudbury, 2000)

HSE. *Essentials of health and safety at work* (third edition with amendments) (HSE Books, Sudbury, 2003)

HSE, free leaflet. *Five steps to risk assessment*, INDG163 (rev. 1) (HSE Books, Sudbury, 2003)

HSE. *Management of health and safety at work: Management of Health and Safety at Work Regulations 1992. Approved Code of Practice*, L21 (HSE Books, Sudbury, 2000)

HSE. *Manual handling. Manual Handling Operations Regulations 1992 – Approved Code of Practice*, L23 (second edition) (HSE Books, Sudbury, 1998)

HSE. *Personal protective equipment at work. Personal Protective Equipment at Work Regulations 1992 – guidance on Regulations*, L25 (HSE Books, Sudbury, 2000)

HSE. *Controlling noise at work. The Control of Noise at Work Regulations 2005. Guidance on Regulations*, L108 (HSE Books, Sudbury, 2005)

HSE. *Work with materials containing asbestos. Control of Asbestos Regulations 2006. Approved Code of Practice and Guidance*, L28 (HSE Books, Sudbury, 2006)

Management of Health and Safety at Work Regulations 1999, SI 1999/3242 (HMSO, London)

Manual Handling Operations Regulations 1992, SI 1992/2793 (HMSO, London)

Control of Noise at Work Regulations 2005, SI 2005/1643 (HMSO, London)

Personal Protective Equipment at Work Regulations 1992, SI 1992/2966 (HMSO, London)

R v Board of Trustees of the Science Museum (9 March 1993), Court of Appeal, 1 WLR 1171 (Times Law Reports, 15 March 1993)

R v Chargot Ltd and others (10 December 2008), House of Lords (2008), UKHL 73

Chapter 6
Controlling risks to health, safety and the environment

"Prevention is better than cure." Desiderius Erasmus 1466–1536

The director's role in supervising management systems

Compliance with the law in the UK is generally sufficient to control risks, but successful companies will want to do more than meet the minimum standards required by legislation. This is particularly true if they are operating in several different countries, where the standards of regulation may vary considerably. Obviously, health and safety and environmental law is quite sophisticated and well developed in Europe, North America and parts of Australasia but less so in the emerging and developing economies of Africa, South America and Asia.

No modern company can accept standards of health and safety and environmental protection in less well-regulated countries that it would not tolerate in the developed world. Such an approach could seriously damage a company's reputation and directors will want to ensure that their business does not suffer from the effects of such double standards. Campaigners rightly seize on such examples as indications of a company's lack of real commitment to the standards it professes. Controversy over globalisation and the export of jobs to developing countries also focuses attention on these matters.

Companies that operate in several countries will soon become aware of the two distinct views of legislation. In Europe, as we have seen, the law tends to set out general duties which are supplemented as necessary by specific regulations. The employer is therefore, in general, left to find a suitable way to comply with the duties laid down by the law. Elsewhere in the world, the laws are often more specific and prescriptive. In producing a health, safety and environmental policy for a multinational company, these differences will mean that the precise formulation in any country will differ in order to meet the specific demands of the law as well as to take account of this fundamental difference in the way legislation is considered. Nonetheless, it will be necessary to ensure that the standard of protection and care is common even if the precise way of reaching that standard will differ. What will not be acceptable is the old-fashioned excuse for dangerous or damaging practices – that they are allowed by national legislation, custom and practice.

Even companies whose operations are confined to the UK will want to understand the way our law links with that of the European Union, as the EU has some overall powers in these areas. Obviously, in the field of environmental protection it is necessary to have Europe-wide laws. Half the air pollution the UK produces is exported to the rest of the EU. Half the air pollution the countries just across the Channel produce is blown across to the UK. So, if we want to improve the quality of our air we have to do it together. Similarly, we cannot clean up our beaches if the Elbe and the Rhine are pouring out filth into the North Sea. Together, we have to have environmental rules that protect us all.

In health and safety there are other considerations. If we are to compete on a level playing field, then the requirements and the enforcement must be reasonably similar. So many of our companies are now operating across our continent that it is sensible to try to have as much in common as possible.

Before we faced up to these issues, regulations on health and safety in Britain were largely made under the 1974 Act, based on initiatives by the HSC. More recently, they have guided Britain's position in the EU, where the UK has played an important role in producing the European Directives which are now being implemented throughout the member states. Key among those was the Framework Directive of 1989 which spawned a cluster of 'daughter' directives commonly known as 'the six pack'.

Under the principle of subsidiarity, member states implement Directives by carrying them into their domestic law and adapting the requirements, within the prescribed bounds, to suit their own national structures. Even so, some opinion formers are saying that there is now too much health and safety law and lately the European Commission has begun to talk about the need for consistent implementation and enforcement of existing legislation rather than creating more. However, at the moment there are still several European initiatives under negotiation, so there will be some further new legislation to take account of (see Part 3, Appendix 7).

Most of this new law is based on good practice. Legislation has become more explicit about the 'how' of health and safety management and provides a detailed overlay to the goal-setting approach of the general duties of the 1974 Act, which remains the principal statute in Britain. The company that has set its sights on continuous improvement in health and safety performance and has established a robust system for the management of all risks should therefore have little to fear from European legislation. Indeed, it has the significant advantage that these common standards contribute towards a level playing field among competitors in the European Single Market. Many other European countries are similarly strict about the enforcement of health and safety laws as we are in the UK, and the rest are fast catching up, although it will undoubtedly be a few years before every one of the new members has fully taken the legislation on board.

Leave it to the experts?

Even so, it is still a great temptation to say that health and safety law is just too complicated, technical and specialist for directors to be troubled with and is therefore best left to the experts. However, the law does lay responsibility on directors. It is they who can be fined or even imprisoned and it is therefore essential that the issues should neither be ignored nor delegated to a health and safety manager, out of sight of the board. However competent the experts, they must feel that they have to keep the board properly informed and that the board takes sufficient interest in the detail, so that it can fulfil its legal duties properly.

Good practice

Management of health and safety should not only be a matter of compliance with legal obligation or the avoidance of penalty. Good companies are keen to improve their performance in health and safety for business reasons. They have seen the cost of a poor record and want to make the savings that good practice can deliver. Although inspectors should always take into account compliance with codes of practice and other published guidance and standards when enforcing the law, successful companies will want to take these principles further in order to reduce accidents and days off work to a minimum. In this case, doing good helps a company to do well.

Plenty of practical help about these standards and recommendations on best practice is to be found on the HSE website, www.hse.gov.uk, and from other organisations (see below and Part 3, Appendix 5).

Occupational safety and health management systems

These days, companies that are serious about keeping risks to their workers under proper control will be approaching their responsibilities systematically and will have established an occupational safety and health management system ('OSHMS'). These have developed over the last 15 or so years in Europe and further afield and their principles are closely related to those of quality management systems (such as ISO 9001) and environmental management systems (such as ISO 14001).

However, it would be a mistake to assume that a company is doing enough for health and safety if it is already following ISO 9001 or 14001 approaches to managing quality and the environment. Not only do they not consider health and safety, but they lack certain key features of occupational safety and health management that are vital. In particular, employee participation and occupational health surveillance are essential elements in avoiding accidents and improving health.

Management systems, whether certificated or not, should be neither paper exercises nor ends in themselves. Effective systems must demonstrate continual improvement in terms of efficacy or efficiency and also need to be supported by a positive culture (ie 'the way we do things round here'). Active involvement by directors is much more likely to turn the proper understanding of these issues into a source of profit and the avoidance of loss, rather than a mechanistic reliance on meeting international standards.

HSG65

Companies which have benefited from an effective programme of management of health and safety issues have provided the case studies on which the HSE has based a useful handbook, 'Successful health and safety management' (HSG65, from HSE Books). This publication builds on the HSE's experience and establishes a five-step, cyclical management system:

- set your policy
- organise to implement your policy and improve performance
- plan priorities and objectives, assessing risks and allocating resources
- monitor progress and measure performance
- review and audit the whole system and strengthen it where necessary.

For many companies in Britain and abroad, HSG65 has become the occupational safety and health management textbook of first choice. Its principles remain topical and valid today. For companies operating in Britain, following the advice it contains will generally be recognised by the enforcing authorities as following good practice. More importantly, it should enable a company to reduce significantly its losses through accidents and absenteeism.

Other standards for occupational safety and health management

The British Standards Institution took matters further when it introduced its BS 8800 guidelines (updated in 2004) and then replaced these in 2008 with its BS 18004 guidance for helping companies to integrate the management of occupational safety and health with other elements of business performance, by sharing common management system principles with quality management and environmental management. A further step was taken with the establishment of a means of third-party verification and certification by accredited independent bodies, detailed in the Occupational Health and Safety Assessment Series (OHSAS) 18001 and OHSAS 18002. Not every company will wish to complete the entire process of achieving certification, particularly where it is not a statutory requirement, but some may judge it appealing to potential customers. These standards are not mandatory in Britain but many companies use them to provide a formal structure on which to build a sound approach to managing risks at work. The key features remain broadly those first presented in HSG65, all of which require an audit:

- policy
- organising
- planning and implementing
- monitoring performance
- review.

The following chapters discuss these elements so that a director can ensure that those responsible for implementing the company health and safety policy and programme have properly grasped the essential issues.

For those who want to delve further, there are many other useful sources of technical information and advice on health and safety management. In addition to the Institution of Occupational Safety and Health, the Royal Society for the Prevention of Accidents, the British Safety Council, the International Institute of Risk and Safety Management, the Confederation of British Industry, the Engineering Employers' Federation, the Institute of Directors, the Trades Union Congress, the European Agency for Safety and Health at Work in Bilbao and the International Labour Organization in Geneva have all published relevant material and your expert health and safety practitioner should be familiar with most of these sources.

Action

A director will want to ensure that:

- the board has recorded and communicated its attitude to health and safety and its expectations from its health and safety programme
- the board has clearly defined that it intends to go beyond compliance and seek a standard of health and safety which will deliver cost savings in accident prevention and reduction in days lost
- the board sees health and safety as a business risk to be managed
- the board recognises that it needs to know how well the company is managing health and safety and that it cannot rely on others – however expert – to absolve it from its legal liability and obligation to uphold the company's reputation.

References and further reading

British Standards Institution. *BS 18004:2008 Guide to occupational health and safety management* (BSI Publications, London, 2008)

British Standards Institution. *BS OHSAS 18001:2007 Occupational health and safety management systems requirement standard* (BSI Publications, London, 2007)

Health and Safety at Work etc Act 1974, Ch 37 (HMSO, London)

HSE. *Successful health and safety management*, HSG65 (HSE Books, Sudbury, 2003)

HSE and the Institute of Directors, free leaflet. *Leading health and safety at work*, INDG417 (HSE Books, Sudbury, 2007)

Institution of Occupational Safety and Health, free document. *Business risk management – getting health and safety firmly on the agenda* (IOSH, Leicester, 2008)

Institution of Occupational Safety and Health, free document. *Joined-up working: an introduction to integrated management systems* (IOSH, Leicester, 2006)

Institution of Occupational Safety and Health, free document. *Making a difference – a basic guide to environmental management for OSH practitioners* (IOSH, Leicester, 2009)

Institution of Occupational Safety and Health, free document. *Systems in focus – guidance on OSH management systems* (IOSH, Leicester, 2009)

International Institute of Risk and Safety Management, www.iirsm.org

International Labour Organization. *Guidelines on occupational safety and health management systems* (ILO, Geneva, 2001)

International Organization for Standardization. *ISO 9001:2008 Quality management systems.* (ISO, Geneva, 2008; www.iso.org)

International Organization for Standardization. *ISO 14001:2004 Environmental management systems.* (ISO, Geneva, 2004; www.iso.org)

Management of Health and Safety at Work Regulations 1999, SI 1999/3242 (HMSO, London)

Chapter 7
Policy – setting the framework

"All injuries and occupational illnesses can be prevented. At DuPont, we believe that this is a realistic goal and not just a theoretical objective. Our safety performance proves that this is achievable, as we have plants with over 1,000 employees that operated for over 10 years without a lost-time injury." DuPont

Policy sets the direction in which the board wishes the company to go. The same mistakes that cause injuries and illness also lead to property damage, pollution and the interruption of production, so a safety, health and environmental policy must aim to minimise and control all accidental loss and environmental damage. Procedures such as identifying hazards and assessing risks, deciding what precautions are needed, putting them into place and checking that they are being used to protect people, improve quality and safeguard plant, production and the community outside. Inevitably there will also be a need for clear and comprehensive documentation of risk assessments, operating procedures and so on.

In Britain, every employer of five or more people is legally obliged to have a written health and safety policy. The law does not prescribe what the policy should contain, but it needs to make clear what the company aims to achieve and how it will do it. At the very least it must convey to employees the board's commitment to compliance with health and safety law. There is no such mandatory demand for an environmental policy at present but most companies will recognise that such a statement is important if they are to meet their growing environmental obligations.

The high level policy statement
The high level policy statement, which needs to be authorised by the board and signed by the chief executive, should be seen as the driver for improvement throughout the company. As such, it will not have to spell out detailed policies that will be more appropriate in the office, plant or divisional statements where references to manuals of safe operating practice, standards, data sheets and

written procedures are to be expected. By contrast, this high level document will be the board's policy statement setting the vision and making clear the commitment, responsibilities and accountabilities.

A typical high level statement might be set out quite briefly along these lines:

> The board is committed to ensuring the protection of our employees from risks to their health and safety and of the community at large from risks to the environment. We aim to set and maintain standards of health, safety and environmental performance across the company which will ensure your health and safety at work and the health and safety of others who may be affected by our work activities, as well as the protection of the environment that is affected by our operations as a business.
>
> To enable us to do this the board has set the following objectives:
> 1. We will, as a minimum, comply with all relevant health, safety and environmental legislation and industry standards and, wherever reasonably practicable, seek to adopt best practice
> 2. We will provide visible leadership, leading by example and considering the health, safety and environmental implications of all our strategic decisions
> 3. We will ensure continual improvement and the prevention of pollution
> 4. We will organise and maintain effective arrangements for the good management of health, safety and environment throughout the company and engage all our employees in these arrangements
> 5. We will define and communicate everyone's health, safety and environmental responsibilities and required competencies clearly
> 6. We will monitor our health, safety and environmental performance and review our systems for managing performance regularly

7. We will ensure that risks to the health, safety and environment of our employees and others who may be affected are properly assessed and controlled, including our contractors and suppliers

8. We will consult our employees and ensure that competent advice and suitable training and resources are made available to assist them in performing their duties to promote health, safety and environmental protection

9. We will report annually to you on our performance.

Signed: Chief Executive

Date:

Date of next review:

These are the fundamentals of a statement of general company policy on health, safety and environmental protection. It can be accompanied by an inspirational mission statement, if that chimes with the company's corporate culture. But fashions in management change rapidly and these things can be overdone. A health, safety and environmental policy needs to be rooted in day-to-day business reality and earn the trust of the workforce.

Divisional or plant level policies

In a large company with several divisions and separate operating sites, particularly if it operates in different countries with differing regulatory regimes, the board's intentions expressed in its general policy statement will need to be reflected in policies at divisional or plant level. These are the vehicles for more detail, with references to operating procedures, manuals and standards, explaining who does what, when and how. These local policies should cover at least the following key points, specifically naming responsible individuals, locations and timescales:

Responsibilities

- Overall and direct responsibility is held by (name)
- Day to day responsibility is held by (name)
- Individuals responsible for areas are (name)
- Responsibilities of employees are (define)

Risks

- Risk assessments will be undertaken by (name)
- Findings will be recorded and reported to (name)
- Remedial action is to be approved by (name)
- Action is to be taken by (name)
- Action is to be checked by (name)
- Assessments will be reviewed every (period)

Consultation with employees

- Employee representatives are (name)
- Consultation with employees is provided by (name)

Procurement, plant/equipment and premises

- Health, safety and environmental considerations for all design, procurement and outsourcing are the responsibilities of (name)
- New plant and equipment will be checked by (name)
- Maintenance of premises (including asbestos management and security) is the responsibility of (name)
- Maintenance of plant and equipment (including Legionella control) is the responsibility of (name)
- Faulty plant/equipment and premises should be reported to (name)

Hazardous substances
- New substances will be checked for safety by (name)
- COSHH assessments are the responsibility of (name)
- Actions arising from assessments will be taken by (name)
- Assessments will be reviewed by (name)

Information, instruction and supervision
- Health and safety information and advice is available from (name)
- Young or new workers and trainees will be supervised by (name)
- Employees working offsite are given relevant health and safety information by (name)

Competence
- Training needs will be identified by (name)
- Induction training will be given by (name)
- Job-specific training will be given by (name)
- Jobs requiring specific training are (specify)
- Training records are kept by (name)
- Competence of contractors will be checked by (name)
- Induction of contractors will be performed by (name)

Injuries and ill health
- First aid medical attention is available at (place)
- Appointed first aiders are (name)
- Accidents, diseases and dangerous occurrences are recorded and reported to the enforcing authority by (name)
- Health surveillance is arranged by (name)
- Jobs requiring health surveillance are (specify)

Monitoring
- Workplace inspections and audits take place every (period)
- Incidents, including near misses and those causing injury, ill health or environmental harm, are investigated by (name)
- Sickness absence is monitored by (name)
- Meetings of the safety committee take place every (period)
- Reports are submitted to management every (period)
- Performance and behaviour of contractors is the responsibility of (name)

Emergency procedures:
- Fire risks are assessed by (name)
- Means of escape are checked by (name)
- Firefighting equipment is maintained by (name)
- Fire alarms and detection equipment are maintained by (name)
- Fire alarms and detection equipment are tested every (period)
- Emergency evacuation drills are practised every (period)
- Business continuity planning and communication is the responsibility of (name)

It is vital to emphasise the reference under 'competence' to contractors and suppliers. Many companies are let down by poor performance on the part of their contractors. There is every reason why they should influence improvement in their contractors' management of health and safety. The company that is paying for their performance can easily be found to be liable when things go wrong. That's why contractors should be included in any arrangements made for safety, health and the environment.

> ! •
>
> Action
>
> Directors will want to ensure that:
>
> • the company has a clearly written policy for health, safety and the environment which specifies who is responsible and the arrangements for identifying hazards and assessing risks and controlling them
> • the board has discussed and authorised such a policy. They will also want to know when it was last reviewed and communicated to managers and the workforce
> • they take every opportunity to make site visits to establish whether the workforce knows about the board's policy, and in particular that worker representatives are fully in the picture. They will also want to find out what workers think of the policy. Communication of the policy is, after all, just as vital as having it in the first place.

References and further reading

Health and Safety at Work etc Act 1974, Ch 37 (HMSO, London)

Health and Safety (Consultation with Employees) Regulations 1996, SI 1996/1513 (HMSO, London)

HSE. *Consulting employees on health and safety: a guide to the law*, INDG232 (HSE Books, Sudbury, 2002)

HSE. *Essentials of health and safety at work* (third edition with amendments) (HSE Books, Sudbury, 2003)

HSE. *Successful health and safety management*, HSG65 (HSE Books, Sudbury, 2003)

HSE and the Institute of Directors, free leaflet. *Leading health and safety at work*, INDG417 (HSE Books, Sudbury, 2007)

Management of Health and Safety at Work Regulations 1999, SI 1999/3242 (HMSO, London)

Safety Representatives and Safety Committees Regulations 1977, SI 1977/500 (HMSO, London)

Chapter 8
Organising for good management of health and safety

"Good health and safety is good business." *Sir Frank Davies, Chairman of the Health and Safety Commission 1994–99*

Organisation of an effective occupational safety and health management system is really the key to successful health and safety management. With the benefit of its experience of many case studies of success and failure, the HSE has defined an effective management system as follows:

- input (uncontrolled hazards and risks)
- process (the occupational safety and health management system)
    - level 1: management arrangements
    - level 2: risk control systems
    - level 3: workplace precautions
- output (controlled hazards and risks)
- outcome (no injuries, no ill health, no incidents, stakeholder satisfaction).

This may seem a simplistic, even idealistic, model but it does capture the essentials. However, as is so often the case, it is necessary to cut through the jargon:

- *input* means identifying all the significant hazards
- *process* is the implementation and active monitoring of the occupational safety and health management system, the heart of which is the risk control system
- *output* is the expected effect of the risk control systems
- *outcomes* are measured by reactive monitoring of incidents (see Chapter 10).

Analysed in this way, it is possible to understand whether or not you have the essential elements of an occupational safety and health management system in place and how it is working. A helpful way of examining your system closely is to imagine it with three identifiable levels:

- level 1 contains the key elements of the health and safety management system: the policy and management arrangements needed to plan and implement the various risk control systems
- level 2, the risk control system, is the bread and butter of the occupational safety and health management system, ensuring that the hazards have been identified and attendant risks have been assessed and adequately controlled
- level 3 means that workplace precautions are in place, maintained and operating effectively.

In order to manage risks effectively employers need the participation of their staff and their commitment and contribution to the OSH management system. This attitude within the company is often referred to as a 'health and safety culture', a phenomenon discussed more fully in Chapter 12.

Nothing will be achieved without visible management commitment. Commitment starts at the top of the organisation. To sow the seeds and reap the benefit of a positive health and safety culture, the board needs to establish and nurture what are sometimes referred to as 'the four Cs':

- control
- co-operation
- communication
- competence.

Precisely what does this jargon mean?

Control
Establishing and maintaining effective control is as vital to the good management

of health and safety as it is for other business functions. There is a need for the board to lead by example, demonstrate top management's commitment and signal clear direction.

The people responsible for particular health and safety functions, for example seeing that risk assessments are reviewed and kept up to date, should be clearly identified. Managers, foremen and supervisors must clearly understand their duties.

Employees must understand their own duties and how these are supervised (they must co-operate with their employer, not endanger themselves or others and use safety equipment correctly).

An important element of control is the setting of performance standards, supported by systems, rules and procedures, so that everyone knows what is expected of them and how to work in a safe and healthy way.

Co-operation

Everyone benefits from employees' co-operation in health and safety management. They and their representatives need to be consulted, particularly when carrying out risk assessments or investigating incidents and learning the lessons from them. Workers often know much more about what goes on in the workplace than senior management. Their knowledge needs to be used to improve health and safety.

Communication

Directors have a duty to provide health and safety information, in particular about hazards, risks and control measures. The board's policy for health and safety, and any significant findings of risk assessments, must be communicated to the workforce. Directors need to know how this has been done and whether there was appropriate involvement of workers.

The health and safety committee on which worker representatives sit with management is a valuable forum for communication and discussion. It can give good feedback on performance. Directors should monitor how active it is.

Competence

Directors have a duty to provide health and safety training. Training to do a job in a safe and healthy way must be provided free of charge. The company needs to assess the skills needed to carry out tasks safely and healthily. Directors ought therefore to ensure that there has been an assessment of training needs.

Careful thought also needs to be given to the sensitive issue of whether your managers and supervisors are really up to their jobs in terms of their health and safety responsibilities. Line managers are the board's front line in implementing their health and safety policy. It is sometimes assumed that they know all about this subject, particularly if they have been promoted from the shop floor. It is easy to think that they must have gained experience even if they have never been trained. The situation is made worse because managers are often reluctant to admit to any weaknesses. It is therefore always dangerous to assume that they have the necessary knowledge, as the first you might know about a problem is when an accident has occurred on their watch. Managers will need health and safety training, and access to expert advice and support. This should be taken account of in the assessment of skills and training needs which should accompany the risk assessment programme.

Employers are required under the Management of Health and Safety at Work Regulations to appoint someone competent to assist them in carrying out their responsibilities, eg for risk assessments. Most sizable companies are likely to employ a professional health and safety practitioner, or even a team of professionals, often reporting to the human resources manager or director. These practitioners will need to have sufficient skills, knowledge, experience and other qualities to undertake the duties required of them.

Such essential attributes should be possessed by Chartered Members or Chartered Fellows of the Institution of Occupational Safety and Health (IOSH) who hold recognised health and safety qualifications, such as a degree or equivalent, and make a formal commitment to Continuing Professional Development.

Sometimes this 'appointed person' is regarded as the 'health and safety manager', particularly if he or she is in charge of a team of experts. This may be misleading and give other managers the impression that the primary responsibility for managing health and safety rests not on themselves but with the health and safety team. That would be wrong. The legal responsibility is clearly with the line manager and the function of the health and safety staff is not to manage but to advise line management and the board.

Health and safety professionals come from a variety of disciplines, from engineering to occupational hygiene, and while an IOSH Chartered Safety and Health Practitioner should bring both broad and deep knowledge of the whole subject of occupational safety and health, sometimes issues may arise where the company needs recourse to a specialist consultancy. Many consultants are themselves members of IOSH specialising in, say, ergonomics or high hazards, but it makes sense to seek assurance that any consultant employed has the necessary qualifications, skills, experience and specific knowledge to advise on the particular issue. Checks should also be made that the appropriate indemnity insurance cover is held. In 2011 the Occupational Safety and Health Consultants Register (OSHCR) was launched by the HSE, supported by a number of safety organisations. The register lists consultants who can offer general advice to UK businesses to help them manage risks to health and safety.

Safety representatives and safety committees

Since 1977, there have been regulations in Great Britain on setting up safety committees and appointing safety representatives. Independent research has shown that in companies where safety committees and trained safety representatives are active, standards of health and safety are higher and performance is improved. They contribute to the development of a positive safety culture – the committee is both a valuable forum for debate between management and workers and an effective channel for communication and feedback.

It is not the employer's responsibility to appoint safety representatives. In Great Britain the law allows recognised trade unions to appoint them from among the employees. The trade unions will normally appoint representatives of a group or groups of workers for whom they have negotiating rights. However, this does not mean that they cannot raise health and safety issues for the workforce as a whole. Where there is no recognised trade union, the management will probably want to appoint worker representatives or, better still, encourage the workforce to choose them for themselves. There are no limitations on the number of representatives that may be appointed but the HSC has given guidance about this and other relevant matters in its approved code of practice and guidance notes, available from HSE Books.

The role of safety representatives

Employers are required to consult with safety representatives about making arrangements for promoting and developing measures to ensure health and safety and checking their effectiveness. Conversely, the safety representatives are required to speak for employees in these consultations. The law prescribes certain functions and rights for safety representatives, though these are not to be regarded as duties. They are to:

- represent the employees in consultations with the employer
- investigate potential hazards and dangerous occurrences and examine the causes of accidents at the workplace
- investigate complaints relating to health and safety by any employee they represent
- make representations to the employer about the above matters
- carry out inspections (discussed in more detail below)
- represent employees in consultations with inspectors
- receive information from inspectors
- attend meetings of the safety committee.

The code of practice approved by the HSC suggests that safety representatives should normally bring to the management's notice in writing any unsafe or unhealthy conditions that come to their attention, though this does not preclude an immediate face-to-face approach for urgent matters or relatively minor concerns. The code of practice also suggests that safety representatives should record when they have made an inspection, and provides a model pro forma which can be copied to the employer to bring matters arising from inspections to his attention. These reports may usefully be discussed by the safety committee.

Safety representatives need to be able to take up any matters with management without delay, and therefore need ready access to the person who has clearly been authorised to act on behalf of management.

Safety representatives must be allowed to take time off with pay to carry out their functions and to undergo training in accordance with the HSC's approved code of practice. Management has to consult safety representatives in good time about:

- any measure it is planning to introduce which may substantially affect health and safety
- arrangements for appointing competent persons under the Management of Health and Safety at Work Regulations
- the health and safety information it is required to give employees
- the planning and organisation of health and safety training for employees
- the consequences for employees' health and safety of planning and introducing new technologies.

Inspections and investigations by safety representatives

Safety representatives must be provided with the facilities and assistance they may reasonably require, including allowing them to carry out workplace inspections and investigate accidents and complaints.

They are required to give reasonable notice of their intention to carry out an inspection, and the code of practice encourages joint inspections by the employer and safety representatives, though this does not prevent them from acting independently or holding private discussions with the employees they represent.

Their inspections can take a number of forms, such as 'safety tours' or general inspections of the workplace, systematic sampling of particular activities, processes or workplace areas, and 'safety surveys'. Where an accident has occurred or a complaint about conditions has been made, investigations may take the form of an inspection of that part of the workplace – providing that it is safe –

and may include examination of machinery and plant. The HSC has expressed the view that in these circumstances the examination's purpose is to find out the causes of the incident, with the possibility of action to prevent a recurrence, and that the approach to the problem should be a joint one between the employer and safety representatives.

It is worth remembering that if an inspector from the enforcing authority decides to conduct an inspection or investigation he or she will certainly wish to meet safety representatives, probably in private, before a closing discussion with the management.

Workplaces in which two or more trade union-appointed safety representatives formally request the setting up of a safety committee must do so within three months of the request. Competent safety representatives can be a great asset to an organisation and their contribution should be welcomed. The experience of companies that successfully gain the co-operation of their workforce and, where applicable, the trade unions, is that the benefits greatly outweigh the costs. Improvements in health and safety show that a flourishing committee and system of safety representatives bring genuine advantages.

In non-unionised firms and workplaces it is worthwhile encouraging the formation of a safety committee, even when this has not been requested by employees, if you are really serious about establishing a positive health and safety culture. Encouraging communication and providing a regular forum for employees to voice their concerns to management and to share their experiences are essential steps towards building trust and improving culture.

The safety committee

If a safety committee is requested you must, by law:

- consult the safety representatives who made the request
- post a notice stating the committee's composition and scope
- establish the committee not later than three months after the request.

The HSC deliberately refrained from prescribing objectives and functions for safety committees but suggested that the main objective would be 'the promotion of co-operation between employers and employees in instigating, developing and carrying out measures to ensure the health and safety at work of the employees'.

The HSC also suggested that functions could include:

- the study of accident and notifiable disease statistics and trends, with reports and recommendations to management for corrective action
- similar examination of safety audit reports
- consideration of reports and information provided by enforcing authorities' inspectors
- consideration of reports by safety representatives
- assisting in developing works safety rules and safe systems of work
- keeping an eye on the safety content of employee training
- monitoring the adequacy of safety-related communication and publicity in the workplace
- providing a link with the enforcing authority.

The number of meetings and the appointment of a chairman are really matters of common sense, although fewer than three or four meetings a year would be unlikely to be sufficient for adequate progression of significant issues. On the other hand, continued meetings with little real business are just as debilitating for serious debate.

There is no legal requirement that lays down who should chair the committee but experience suggests that the willingness of a director to chair the committee not only gives it more status and clout but also makes for a more businesslike and relevant discussion. If the board appointed one of its number as health and safety 'champion', chairing the committee could be seen as part of his or her functions, helping to keep the champion in touch with safety representatives and shop floor health and safety issues as well as providing the committee with a strong link to the board. Joint chairmanship, shared with perhaps the most senior or experienced safety representative, is another model that has worked well, and the role could be rotated between meetings.

Minutes of meetings should be agreed. Copies should be made available and displayed at workplaces, and sent to each safety rep and the most senior manager responsible for health and safety.

The work of the committee should periodically be brought to the attention of the board.

> **Action**
>
> A director will want to ensure that:
>
> - the company is properly organised for managing health and safety
> - managers and supervisors are fully competent in this area
> - the safety representatives are happy with the way things are organised
> - the safety committee is active and useful
> - the chairmanship and organisation of meetings is satisfactory
> - the board receives reports from the committee at reasonable intervals and the committee has access to the board in the event of a serious concern
> - the work of the committee is adequately communicated to the workforce and the management.

References and further reading

Health and Safety (Consultation with Employees) Regulations 1996, SI 1996/1513 (HMSO, London)

HSE. *Safety representatives and safety committees. Safety Representatives and Safety Committees Regulations 1977 – Approved Code of Practice*, L87 (HSE Books, Sudbury, 1996)

HSE. *Successful health and safety management*, HSG65 (HSE Books, Sudbury, 2003)

HSE and the Institute of Directors, free leaflet. *Leading health and safety at work*, INDG417 (HSE Books, Sudbury, 2007)

Safety Representatives and Safety Committees Regulations 1977, SI 1977/500 (HMSO, London)

Management of Health and Safety at Work Regulations 1999, SI 1999/3242 (HMSO, London)

Occupational Safety and Health Consultants Register, www.oshcr.org.

Chapter 9
Planning and implementation – safe systems of work

"Plan, do, check, act." *Dr W Edwards Deming*

Planning

Planning is the first essential step and the key to ensuring that risk management is really going to work. It involves setting objectives, identifying hazards, assessing risks, developing safe systems of work and setting and implementing standards of performance, thus laying the foundations for developing a positive health and safety culture.

Planning should cover identifying hazards and assessing risks (already discussed in Chapter 5), and complying with the health and safety laws which are applicable to the company's business (which means not only the general duties but knowing whether any particular hazards or processes attract special regulations).

To achieve this, objectives and targets need to be agreed with managers, supervisors and workers' representatives. Objectives and targets for improvement need to be SMART (specific, measurable, agreed, realistic and timescaled).

Planning should not overlook other functions which have a bearing on health and safety outcomes, such as purchasing and supply. An important question to ask is: 'Does the purchasing policy take properly into account those risks to health and safety which might be imported into the company?'

The plan should include such matters as the design of specific tasks and processes so that they ensure safe working. Obviously there should also be fully thought-through procedures and systems of work for any potentially hazardous tasks, for example entry into confined spaces where toxic gases could be present, or working at height.

Maintenance activities have proved to be among the most hazardous and in 1992 the HSE published *Dangerous maintenance*, a collection of case studies demonstrating the vital importance of planning these activities with the prevention of accidents in mind. This is the motivation behind the establishment of a 'permit to work' regime, which is an important protection for both workforce and management alike. A permit to work is a document which clearly sets out details of the work to be done, the risk assessment and the precautions which will be taken. Until this document has been authorised by a competent person and issued to those who are to carry out the work, no work should begin. Clearly this is a system which requires rigorous policing by the company's management and it is particularly important where contractors are also involved on site. They must, of course, be fully covered by the regime and trained if necessary.

Emergency and evacuation procedures also need to be planned, if necessary in co-operation with visiting contractors, the fire authority, emergency planning officers of the local authority, and neighbours.

Standards

Planning should include the setting of standards and the provision of appropriate procedures. These must be specific and workable. They should identify who does what, how, when and with what intended result. Statements such as 'staff must be trained' are difficult to implement if no one knows exactly what training is required or who is to do the training.

Some standards are available 'off the shelf' and will represent current good practice in your sector or industry. They will probably have been developed by the relevant trade association, perhaps in association with the regulator, or by one of the HSC's numerous advisory committees, on which employer and employee representatives sit together with experts and representatives of the public interest.

For example, the rubber industry guarding standard for the highly dangerous 'in-running nip' at horizontal two-roll mills has been developed and refined by a joint committee over many years and is accepted by the regulator's inspectors as good practice. It would be folly to divert from the accepted standard for such a potentially dangerous machine. Indeed, this is precisely the kind of issue where a director's liability is best covered by an accepted standard and practice. It is equally true that workers will be reassured to know that management is firmly committed to meeting this standard for their protection.

Some standards have been developed by national or international bodies, eg the British Standards Institution (BSI), European Community (CEN) or International Organization for Standardization (ISO). It is perfectly legitimate for a company to adopt any of these standards as its own, but it needs to be a deliberate act of commitment, effectively communicated to managers and workforce, so that there is no misunderstanding about what is expected. Senior management must take the decisions, of course, but consulting line managers, supervisors and safety representatives during the planning process will pay dividends later when implementing the plan and reviewing progress.

Where industry standards do not exist, the company should set its own, for example for seeing that machinery guarding is regularly checked, cleaning workshops, seeing that ventilation equipment remains efficient, reviewing risk assessments, arranging meetings of the safety committee and so on. Standard-setting is not rocket science and need not always be left to experts.

Health risk management is an even more important area for planning. In the UK over 2 million people believe they suffer from work-related ill health. There are numerous potential causes: exposure to hazardous chemicals, noise, vibration, radiation, high temperatures, humidity, dangerous pathogens, repetitive tasks, lifting heavy loads and stress, to name but some.

The general duties in sections 2 and 3 of the Health and Safety at Work etc Act 1974 require the protection of workers' health and that of any members of the public whose health may be affected by the way your company conducts its undertaking. The Management of Health and Safety at Work Regulations, together with the approved code of practice which explains how to comply with those regulations, set out requirements for assessment of risks, planning, organisation, control, monitoring and review, to prevent ill health. There are in addition several sets of regulations dealing with specific health risks from hazardous substances (such as lead, ionising radiation and asbestos), noise, manual handling and display screen equipment.

Whether it is protection of health or prevention of accidents, directors need to decide what the board's priorities are for improvement of risk control, and declare that they intend to set effective targets. They will wish to consult line managers, workers and supervisors and reach agreement on targets which are stretching but realistically achievable. These can be of many kinds. For example, if the company is badly behind with the risk assessment programme, management should set targets for getting it on track within a reasonable timescale, and allocate the necessary resources. If the issue is noise, then management should ensure that all steps have been taken to reduce noise from plant and processes, that adequate hearing protection is worn, and that when replacement machinery is ordered it is as quiet as possible. If transport accidents are causing concern, it should find out the root causes and set a target for eradication. If slips, trips and falls are increasing, it ought to run a campaign and set a target for reduction.

It is always important to make it clear that the management means business, and that it will provide whatever additional resources it judges necessary, whether these involve time, money, trained staff or consultants. This shows commitment by the board and, properly recorded, would help to demonstrate that commitment to an inspector or tribunal should the question of liability arise. Even without such a situation, the gains from fewer accidents and cases of ill health will more than outweigh the cost of the additional effort.

The director's imperative

Implementation of the plan must first mean that everyone understands the board's priorities and accepts the standards and targets that have been set, from the managing director down to shop floor workers, through managers and supervisors and by engaging the safety representatives.

The prior involvement of safety representatives in the planning process will have helped considerably to gain acceptance at this stage. Directors should explain their role in carrying out the health and safety plan, the benefits it is expected to bring, and make it clear that progress will be closely monitored. They should listen to feedback as time goes on and keep the workforce involved. Success can also be achieved through use of the in-house newsletter or intranet (if there is one) to raise the profile of the plan and let everyone know what it is about.

The board's health and safety champion must not allow the enthusiasm to cool. He or she should lead by example and be seen around the workplace, talking about health and safety, keeping managers and supervisors on their toes, and encouraging those who are really trying. The purpose is to demonstrate that the board is really determined that the company should succeed in improving its health, safety and environmental record.

Actions do speak louder than words, and many a good plan has failed for lack of drive and determination at the implementation stage. Non-executive directors will find it worthwhile nominating one of their number to take a particular interest in these issues so that on site visits he or she can look out for evidence of the practical working of the board's policy and ensure that the discussion of health and safety at board meetings is not merely lip service.

Checking the reality

This stage is vital to ensuring that the company's policy, planning, hazard identification and risk assessment are actually being implemented. Many a policy that looked very good on paper has been found by inspectors to be a hollow sham. Board liability is certainly not properly discharged in such circumstances, nor does a company get the benefits from good health and safety performance. Performance assessment needs to be both active and reactive. This is discussed in more detail in Chapter 10. At this stage in the cycle it is possible to review performance and take corrective actions towards improvement.

> **Action**
>
> Directors will want to ensure that:
>
> - they know who is responsible for health and safety planning and for setting standards
> - they understand how the company's planning system works
> - they are clear what sorts of standards have been adopted, and whether these are current good practice
> - they look for evidence of the plan being implemented. Are the targets you have set understood by managers and supervisors? Are they being met?
> - they are clear what the workers and safety representatives think about the policy and its implementation.

References and further reading

HSE. *Successful health and safety management*, HSG65 (HSE Books, Sudbury, 2003)

HSE and the Institute of Directors, free leaflet. *Leading health and safety at work*, INDG417 (HSE Books, Sudbury, 2007)

British Standards Institution. *BS 18004:2008 Guide to occupational health and safety management* (BSI Publications, London, 2008)

International Labour Organization. *Guidelines on occupational safety and health management systems*, ILO-OSH (ILO, Geneva, 2001)

Management of Health and Safety at Work Regulations 1999, SI 1999/3242 (HMSO, London)

Chapter 10
Monitoring

"Your measurement systems will determine what your staff will pay attention to…" Peter F Drucker

Let's assume that the plan has been made and implemented. The next essential element is monitoring performance. Health and safety is like anything else the board sets out to do – it needs a measure of its success. Board members need to know where they are, where they want the firm to be, the strategy for getting there, and the timescale and any targets set.

Monitoring enables the board to tell whether or not the company is on track to meet the targets it has set for health and safety. The high-level aim is to provide the board with information on:

- how the health and safety management system is operating in practice
- whether progress towards targets is being achieved and whether the board's strategy is succeeding
- areas where improvement is necessary.

The measurement system should also provide managers, supervisors, safety representatives and the safety committee with the data they need to play their part in executing the health and safety plan.

Companies tend to find that measurement is one of the more difficult aspects of occupational safety and health management. This is because the main criterion for success is an absence of outcomes such as injuries and ill health, fires and explosions, damage to plant and equipment, rather than tangible growth through burgeoning sales figures, acquisitions and mergers, and other measures of business success.

Directors are usually very familiar with measuring company performance positively in terms of percentage profit on capital employed, market share or return on investment, but are often familiar only with injury and ill health statistics as a measure of success (or failure) in controlling risks to health and safety. Injury and ill health statistics are certainly one valid measure, but they are only a part of the whole picture, and could be regarded as negative outcomes. Indeed, there are a number of drawbacks with injury and ill health statistics:

- injuries and ill health are outcomes of events, not causes. Focusing on root causes of incidents enables the correct preventive measures to be taken, whereas hoping that the numbers of injuries will come down by concentrating on the statistics is misguided
- the difference between an injury and a near miss is often a matter of sheer chance, perhaps measurable in millimetres or microseconds. An injury is merely one consequence of an event which could have been much more severe. The collapse of the tunnel under construction at Heathrow Airport mercifully resulted in no injuries at all but could have had catastrophic consequences for workers, the public and the aviation industry. It was certainly catastrophic in economic terms, causing major transport disruption. The tunnelling contractors were fined £1.2 million for breaching health and safety law, reflecting the judge's view of the measure of the failure of safety management
- if the main risks in a company are from major hazards and potentially catastrophic consequences, it would be dangerous to assume that a low injury and ill health rate means that these risks are under effective control
- putting all the emphasis on the importance of injury and ill health statistics within the company as the principal measure of success has been known to lead to deliberate under-reporting and cover-ups, particularly when the

figures are linked to reward systems. Equally, temporarily increased rates may be due to improved reporting

- there is often a time lag between exposure to a health hazard and the onset of an occupational disease, so this will indicate previous poor performance (though it may still be happening), possibly dating back many years
- a low injury or ill health rate is good but focusing only on this can lead to complacency. Using several, different kinds of measures will paint a clearer picture of how well the company is doing.

Many organisations have therefore struggled to develop performance measures which are not simply based on injury and ill health statistics. This is difficult as it is not a matter of simply taking performance measures 'off the shelf'. Measures that chime well with a company's existing culture are more likely to be accepted by management and the workforce, and may therefore be better developed in house.

Active monitoring (before things go wrong) involves regular inspection and checking to ensure that standards are being implemented and maintained, and that management controls are working. *Reactive monitoring* (after things go wrong) involves learning from mistakes.

It is not yet an explicit statutory requirement for all companies to investigate their own accidents, cases of disease and dangerous occurrences and to produce reports but, as we mentioned before, in 2001 the HSC consulted on this future possibility.

Reactive monitoring is important and companies which are serious about health and safety will ensure that every incident, whether or not it causes injury, is investigated to get at the root cause and ensure that it cannot happen again. Sadly, too many people rely on reactive monitoring alone: this is like trying to drive your car by looking only in the mirror at what has already happened, rather than looking ahead to avoid trouble.

Key performance indicators

The HSE has commissioned research into the kind of KPIs for health and safety performance which investment institutions might regard as significant. These are emerging along the following lines:

- whether a director has been appointed as a health and safety 'champion'
- the level of reporting of health and safety management systems
- the number of fatalities
- the lost time injury rate
- the absenteeism rate
- the cost of health and safety losses.

Other KPIs might well include:

- having an up-to-date health and safety policy, signed by the chief executive
- training of key personnel
- keeping data on accidents, ill health and lost time
- keeping risk assessments up to date
- reporting on health and safety performance in company reports
- benchmarking with other companies.

The important thing is for a company to choose KPIs that are measurable, start collecting appropriate data and then analyse them to measure trends in performance. The HSE has also been developing a health and safety performance management index. This online Corporate Health and Safety

Performance Index (CHaSPI) is intended for use by organisations employing more than 250 in the UK and was launched in July 2005. There is also a simpler tool, known as 'the Indicator' or 'Health and Safety Performance Indicator', developed for SMEs.

Action

Directors will want to ensure that:

- the board knows how well the company is performing in health and safety and that there is a clear means of giving the board this information
- KPIs have been set to enable effective monitoring
- standards set by the board are being actively measured
- accurate records are kept of every incident that causes injury, ill health, loss or damage
- there is proper assessment of the costs of these incidents to the company
- they are in a position to say 'We are proud of this performance and prepared to tell the world.'

References and further reading

Global Reporting Initiative, *Sustainability reporting guidelines on economic, environmental and social performance* (GRI, Boston, USA, 2002)

HSE. *A guide to measuring health and safety performance* (HSE Books, Sudbury, 2001)

HSE. Corporate Health and Safety Performance Index (CHaSPI), www.chaspi.info-exchange.com (2005)

HSE. Health and Safety Performance Indicator (HSPI) for small and medium-sized enterprises, www.hspi.info-exchange.com (2005)

HSE and the Institute of Directors, free leaflet. *Leading health and safety at work*, INDG417 (HSE Books, Sudbury, 2007)

Institution of Occupational Safety and Health, free document. *Systems in focus – guidance on OSH management systems* (IOSH, Leicester, 2009)

Measuring health and safety performance (HSE Books, 2001)

Management of Health and Safety at Work Regulations 1999, SI 1999/3242 (HMSO, London)

Chapter 11
Auditing, reviewing and reporting

"If the audit has become the yardstick by which financial performance is measured then the safety audit should become the yardstick by which safety performance is measured. Only with such a management tool can the board, and hence the general public, be satisfied that all aspects of safety are maintained at the right level." *Desmond Fennell, Report of Investigation of the King's Cross fire*

Auditing

Having got the system in place, properly planned, implemented and monitored, it is important to see that it is regularly audited. Although auditing is more commonly associated with financial management and control, it has a strong role to play in allowing the board to check whether the health and safety policy is really being executed on the shop floor. All management systems deteriorate over time or become obsolete as a result of change. Auditing helps managers identify and rectify faults in the system. A company that is striving for continual improvement will be auditing and reviewing performance regularly.

Safety auditing has been defined by the Organisation for Economic Co-operation and Development (OECD) as a 'methodical in-depth examination of all or part of a total operating system with relevance to safety'. It involves planned and documented activity performed in accordance with written procedures to verify, by examination and evaluation of objective evidence, that the appropriate elements of a health and safety system have been developed, documented and implemented.

Although the old style of checklist audit remains valid and useful, the above approach, by concentrating on the regular assessment of the adequacy of management and safety systems in a structured way, provides an essential safeguard to the director. It involves:

- selecting a competent auditor or audit team
- preparation – defining who and what is to be audited and how
- fieldwork – examining documents, interviewing staff and evaluating physical conditions

- writing an audit report
- presenting the report to decision makers
- implementing the recommendations
- reviewing their effect.

Accident prevention can benefit from examining yesterday's incidents but it is essentially about preventing tomorrow's. This is particularly vital in high hazard activities where the frequency of accidents may be quite low but each incident carries with it the potential for catastrophic loss, such as on oil rigs, petrochemical and nuclear sites or mass transport systems. Managers need active systems to provide them with reliable indicators that the risks within their organisations are being adequately controlled and that their safety policies are achieving their objectives. Auditing fulfils this role and provides essential feedback to management that what they intend to be done is actually being done. Again, 'what gets measured gets done'.

Auditing is, of course, only part of safety management and to manage safety properly companies need first to develop a safety management system and apply it. Only then can the system be audited. The audit should test every element of the system: policy, organisation, planning and implementation, measuring and review.

Auditing normally involves sampling of part of the process rather than comprehensive coverage of every issue. For that reason it would be a serious mistake to think that simply remedying deficiencies exposed by auditing is all that is needed. While any reduction in risk is to be welcomed, such a minimal approach is fundamentally flawed and could be positively dangerous. As we have seen, good health and safety management needs to be based on the identification of hazards, objective assessment of the risks and implementation of measures to eliminate or control them. Auditing does not do this on its own. It searches for and identifies areas for improvement and thereby supports the process of overall health and safety management.

Properly trained and experienced auditors, whether from the firm's own staff or competent outsiders, are needed to fulfil the safety auditing role effectively, but there is no reason why the function should not be properly integrated with other audit functions. The important thing is to ensure that the board is made aware of key findings and recommendations and backs remedial actions with its authority.

Auditing brings rigour to the assessment of the system. Audits complement monitoring by looking to see whether the policy, organisation and systems are actually achieving the results desired by the board. Firms need to learn from their experiences. The audit process requires the board to review the effectiveness of their risk management systems and decide how to improve performance, paying attention to the degree of compliance achieved with health and safety standards, including legislation, areas where standards are absent or inadequate, achievement of stated objectives within given timescales, and injury, illness and incident data. This helps to give directors confidence that they have taken reasonable steps to protect their workforce from injury or sickness and themselves from liability.

Reviewing

Monitoring performance (described in Chapter 10), complemented by auditing, enables companies to review their activities and decide how best to improve policy, systems and attitudes towards health and safety within the company, particularly if the review process is pursued with transparency and openness through discussion with managers, employees and their representatives. The information needed for effective reviewing of performance is also the kind of material that companies are being encouraged to disclose; it also aids accountability.

Reporting on performance is a key element in maintaining control of risks. Regular reviews of policy, risk assessments and the effectiveness of your occupational safety and health management systems make good business sense. Businesses move on, and systems begin to atrophy. Conditions change, new plant and materials are acquired, older equipment deteriorates and needs more maintenance, new processes are introduced, key workers leave and new staff are hired, and the process of change means that the systems that once protected health, safety and the environment are no longer adequate. Health and safety standards are not static and companies should be alive to improved control measures and developments in best practice.

The fire at Hickson and Welch Ltd in Castleford, which killed five workers in 1992, the worst accident at a UK chemical plant since Flixborough in 1974, was in part the result of lack of 'corporate memory', which led personnel into fundamental errors and incorrect assumptions in the cleaning of a distillation vessel. The company was prosecuted for breach of the general duty in the 1974 Act to ensure health and safety and fined £250,000 with £150,000 costs. Among the main recommendations of a report subsequently published by the HSE was the statement that 'safe systems of work covering all aspects of operation and maintenance of all process plant should be established and defined in comprehensive instructions including those operations conducted at infrequent intervals. These systems should be monitored by management and reviewed at appropriate intervals.' This advice has become ever more important as modern employment patterns mean that 'corporate memory' is so much rarer than it used to be.

Reviewing should be a continuous rather than a one-off process, with regular reports to the board. The board should say when it expects to receive reports, how often, and what they should contain. It should be someone's designated task to analyse data, brief the health and safety champion and take responsibility for seeing that these reports are delivered on time and put on the board's agenda for discussion and action, not just for noting 'below the line'.

Divisional and plant managers should also be demanding and seeing reports regularly, and they should be discussed with safety representatives on the safety committee. These plant level reports are often produced by the health and safety practitioner, if such a person is employed. They should not overlook input from the medical centre or the works nurse.

Reporting: incidents

Employers are required by law to report certain kinds of accidents, dangerous occurrences or cases of disease to the enforcing authority. These are defined in the Reporting of Injuries, Diseases and Dangerous Occurrences Regulations 1995 (RIDDOR), discussed below. At the national level, this information enables the enforcing authority to identify the industries where risks are arising and to investigate serious accidents. The HSE publishes annually the national figures, broken down in various ways, and these statistics are worth studying as they cast light on the kind of risks that should be of concern at company level. Using the company's reporting information properly gives a useful mechanism for helping to check the efficacy of the system.

RIDDOR requires the following kinds of incident to be reported (this list is illustrative, not exhaustive, and full information can be found in the guide to the regulations available from HSE Books):

- death or major injury
- over three-day injury
- work-related disease
- dangerous occurrences.

Death or major injury
Major injuries include work-related:

- fractures
- amputations
- dislocations
- loss of sight (temporary or permanent)
- eye injuries
- acute illness requiring medical treatment
- loss of consciousness arising from absorption of a substance by inhalation, ingestion or through the skin
- injury from electric shock.

If there is an accident connected with work and your employee or a self-employed person is killed or suffers a major injury (including as a result of physical violence), or if a member of the public is killed or taken to hospital, your company must notify the enforcing authority without delay, eg by telephone, and follow this up within 10 days by sending a completed accident form (F2508).

Over-three-day injury
An over-three-day injury is one which is not major but results in the injured person being away from work or being unable to do their normal work for more than three days, including non-work days.

Disease

Certain diseases are reportable to the enforcing authority, such as:

- occupational dermatitis
- skin cancer and other occupational cancers
- lung diseases including occupational asthma, pneumoconiosis, asbestosis and mesothelioma
- certain infections such as anthrax, hepatitis, tuberculosis, tetanus, legionellosis and leptospirosis
- certain poisonings
- decompression sickness
- hand–arm vibration syndrome
- certain musculoskeletal disorders.

If a doctor notifies you that your employee is suffering from a reportable work-related disease your company must report this to the enforcing authority by completing and sending form F2508A.

Dangerous occurrences

Dangerous occurrences are serious events which have not resulted in a reportable injury but clearly could have done. These include incidents such as:

- the collapse or overturning of a crane
- electrical short circuit or overload causing fire or explosion
- accidental release of a biological agent likely to cause severe human illness
- explosion, collapse or bursting of closed vessels or associated pipework
- collapse of a scaffold more than 5 metres high.

These events have to be reported immediately, eg by telephone, and followed up by sending form F2508A within 10 days. As a result of a recent review of RIDDOR, the HSE has announced its intention to move in September 2011 to a predominantly online system, with a suite of seven forms available on its website to make the statutory reporting process quicker and easier. The HSE's Infoline telephone information service will close.

Companies which are serious about managing their risks will be using this information themselves and investigating every incident, whether or not the enforcing authority decides to do so. Some companies will be going further than the law requires and ensuring that all incidents causing lost time or damage are notified internally. Some will go so far as to require near misses to be notified internally, particularly if they are experiencing few injury-causing incidents, to enable them to investigate the circumstances of a near miss, establish root causes and take preventive measures to avoid recurrence of circumstances that might cause injury or damage next time. Such processes provide, in addition, a useful check on the efficacy of fundamental health and safety arrangements.

Reporting: performance

One of the action points in 'Revitalising health and safety' was for all public bodies to summarise their health and safety performance and plans in their annual reports, starting no later than 2000/2001. Greater emphasis is now being placed by the government and investors on disclosure in company reports of many aspects of performance – not just financial, but also those covered by corporate social responsibility.

Health and safety is no exception to this pressure, though it is not yet a statutory requirement to include this field in annual reports. The UK government has made clear that it will review the necessity for mandatory reporting after assessing the response to a 'challenge' issued in 2001 by the minister and the chair of the HSC to the top 350 companies in Britain. The challenge requested that they should voluntarily set targets for improvement of health and safety, and report progress in their annual reports. However, it seems only to be a matter of time before regulatory action is taken to force this disclosure, particularly as the government has already recommended this for public bodies.

The proper question is, therefore: why wait? Dealing with accidents is an expensive business. High standards result in a real reputational gain and a real advantage to the bottom line. There is nothing to fear from the regulator by declaring a company's present position and describing how continual improvement in this important area of corporate social responsibility is to be achieved. Indeed, there are real benefits in disclosure. Company annual reports provide an opportunity for companies to give a positive description of their performance in managing significant risks, including health and safety risks, in which investment fund managers, insurers and the like are taking an increased interest. A greater appreciation of the wider importance of risk management is raising the significance of this information for the financial community.

How to report
Three levels of reporting are practicable, according to guidance published by the Institution of Occupational Safety and Health (IOSH). These are Level 1 (minimal), Level 2 (comprehensive internal) and Level 3 (external).

Level 1 should be attempted by all organisations and simply comprises a section in the annual published report signed off by the directors. It will cover at least workplace injuries and ill health, shown as fatalities, major injuries and lost time incidents. The data may be presented as frequency rates rather than simply raw numbers of incidents, as this enables comparisons with past performance and with company, sector and national averages and targets.

The report should also contain information about total days lost: these statistics shed light on the severity of injury and ill health suffered and the effectiveness of rehabilitation.

National targets have now been set in the government's strategy documents 'Revitalising health and safety' and 'Securing health together' (see Chapter 1 for more information) and comments could be included on the company's contribution to achieving these targets. It is a positive step to include in the report any information about awards won, number of days without a lost time incident and the like. It will also be seen as honest to include any negative information about enforcement action against the company such as improvement or prohibition notices or prosecutions, or about compensation claims settled.

Level 2 reports are much more comprehensive internal reports, covering detailed statistics and other performance indicators, trends analysis, and comment about successes or failures at divisional or plant levels. Internal reporting is the most commonly found, as many companies think perhaps that this is private grief best kept from the public gaze. However, growing pressures for disclosure and recognition of transparency as a sign of a positive culture are making it difficult to justify not producing a public document.

Level 3 reports are public reports which are produced in the context of CSR reporting, for which the Global Reporting Initiative has issued guidelines.

The Companies Act 2006

Government policy on reporting continues to evolve, but not always along expected lines. New reporting regulations introduced by the Department of Trade and Industry in 2005 would have required British 'quoted companies' to prepare an Operating and Financial Review (OFR) and all other companies except eligible small companies to expand their directors' reports to include a Business Review. The Accounting Standards Board issued an accompanying reporting standard (RS1). Compliance with that standard would have been deemed to be effective compliance with mandatory reporting requirements.

However, in late 2005, the Chancellor announced the government's intention to scrap the requirement for quoted companies to prepare an OFR. The regulations were revoked in January 2006 before they came fully into effect.

Directors of quoted companies are now required under the Companies Act 2006 to provide a 'business review' or a voluntary OFR describing key performance indicators and risks to the company's business, including information on environmental matters and the company's employees. The Accounting Standards Board has converted its standard RS1 into a Reporting Statement, giving best practice guidance on voluntary reporting.

Looking ahead

It is also worth thinking about arranging an annual board discussion about the health and safety issues coming over the horizon. The discussion might usefully be structured along the following lines, testing the company's ability to cope with both present and future challenges, such as:

Regulatory trends

- goal-setting law replacing prescription, with risk assessment the means to the end (risk control)
- greater competence expected
- greater worker involvement expected, including rights to inspect and investigate
- supply chain management – responsibility for the standards of contractors and suppliers
- accountability – the legal requirement for an OFR
- corporate killing – companies to be liable for manslaughter if causing death at work

Litigation

- changing public attitudes towards risk and redress
- the 'compensation culture', 'ambulance chasing' and 'no win, no fee' claims

Business and reputation management

- increasing institutional shareholder pressure
- corporate social responsibility seen to include health and safety best practice
- key performance indicators being developed

Health

- concerns about work-related stress, violence and bullying
- exposure to asbestos, carcinogens and other long-term liabilities

Questions for the board

- how well are we prepared?
- what more do we need to do?

Action

Directors will need to know:

- whether their company operates a health and safety audit system
- whether the system involves staff at all levels of the company, including the board
- what action is taken on the findings of audit
- what kind of performance monitoring their company is undertaking
- whether the information about health and safety performance is made available internally and/or externally, and how
- whether that information is summarised in the company report to shareholders
- what action the board expects to be taken in the light of the information.

References and further reading

Accounting Standards Board. *Reporting Statement: Operating and Financial Review* (ASB Publications, London, 2006) – available online at www.frc.org.uk/images/uploaded/documents/Reporting%20Statements%20OFR%20web.pdf

Companies Act 2006, Ch 46 (HMSO, London)

Global Reporting Initiative. *Sustainability reporting guidelines* (GRI, Boston, USA, 2002)

HSE. *Successful health and safety management*, HSG65 (HSE Books, Sudbury, 2003)

HSE and the Institute of Directors, free leaflet. *Leading health and safety at work*, INDG417 (HSE Books, Sudbury, 2007)

Institution of Occupational Safety and Health, free document. *Reporting performance – guidance on including health and safety performance in annual reports* (IOSH, Leicester, 2008)

Reporting of Injuries, Diseases and Dangerous Occurrences Regulations 1995, SI 1995/3163 (HMSO, London)

Sustainability reporting guidelines on economic, environmental and social performance (GRI, Boston, USA, 2001)

Turnbull, N. *Internal control: guidance for directors on the Combined Code* (Institute of Chartered Accountants in England and Wales, London, 1999)

Chapter 12
Safety culture, reputation and reward

"Have regard for your name, since it will remain for you longer than a great store of gold." The Apocrypha, Ecclesiasticus 41.12

'How we do things around here' is an oft-quoted definition of company culture. However, the saying does not always bring positive overtones. A major international civil engineering project, the Channel Tunnel, was beset by problems as the culture became a negative one of production at any cost. Macho management of the tunnelling operation almost spelt disaster for the whole project. After several fatal accidents, prosecutions and heavy fines, all amid the glare of adverse publicity and causing major costly delay and disruption, the project was only put back on track by replacing managers, retraining the workforce and thus changing the culture.

Employees quickly catch on to what really matters to senior management. If health and safety is not among the management's priorities, resentment, demotivation and disloyalty soon follow. The 'whistleblower' culture that developed in the 1990s would not have been necessary if all companies had shown commitment and been honest and open with their employees. Communicating the vision and then 'walking the talk' are key responsibilities of senior managers.

There are ways to assess the state of your company's culture. Simply talking to employees, particularly the safety representatives, is a very good method. Being seen by the workforce around the workplace really counts when it comes to showing the board's commitment to safety.

Involvement of safety representatives can contribute enormously to the growth of a positive culture. Confident managers realise that experienced workers know a lot more than they do about running the plant, and therefore set out quite deliberately to exploit this knowledge as a resource. If your plant or premises become the subject of an inspection by the enforcing authority, be assured that the inspector will be drawing on that very same knowledge.

In addition to this informal procedure, there are some more sophisticated methods, such as the use of staff attitude surveys, usually done by questionnaire, and 'climate assessment' tools, which can be helpful to management in focusing on what needs to be improved. Publishing the results of attitude surveys helps build trust between management and the workforce.

Companies that manage health and safety well are generally successful, profitable businesses. Some firms like DuPont have worked for over a century to establish and maintain their well-deserved international reputation for safety. The best performing chemical companies in the UK aspire to reach their standards, and respect DuPont's achievement. It is perhaps no surprise to learn that, in that company, unsafe practices such as walking down stairs carrying bags in both hands are severely frowned on and disciplined. The chairman spends time every day giving active leadership on safety, even getting his driver to check the equipment in the car boot before setting off on a journey. Examples like this can mean a lot, and are plainly evident where a strong 'safety culture' exists. The HSE has recently published a series of case studies demonstrating the vital role that director leadership has to play in ensuring that risks are properly managed. The studies highlight the benefits that leadership brings both to employee health and safety and the business.

Such a culture was once a rarity. The Forth rail bridge was built between 1883 and 1890 at the cost of nearly 80 lives. The toll from mining disasters was even greater. In those days society accepted that major civil engineering projects would take a heavy toll in lives, and it was a general rule of thumb, for example, that a tunnel would cost at least one life for every mile of tunnel driven. Today that attitude would be utterly intolerable, and the building of the Queen Elizabeth Bridge over the Thames at Dartford, and the Second Severn Crossing at Bristol, have shown that major projects can be completed successfully without the loss of a single life.

Yet changing a culture is very difficult and we must accept that it may take quite a long time to make really significant improvements. But be encouraged by the way in which the poor safety performance of the Channel Tunnel construction project was turned round by a determined management.

Reputation and reward

Corporations gain reputations for being good or bad employers, or more generally good or bad companies. A bad reputation is difficult to shake off, but a good reputation, having taken a long time to build, can be lost by a single catastrophic failure. Similarly, an accumulation of lesser events can lead employees and commentators to question a company's competence and focus on the responsibility of the board. The British media are quick to pillory failure of any kind, particularly if big companies with household names are involved.

We are working within a national culture that has made significant improvements to safety at work and Britain generally enjoys a good reputation abroad. By 2009/10, fatal accidents at work in Great Britain were at their lowest recorded level. Nevertheless, there is no room for complacency; as recently as 2003/04, 236 people, including both employees and self-employed workers, were killed at work in Britain, and another 30,000 suffered major injuries. Roughly 130,000 suffer an injury resulting in more than three days off work. Over a million workers suffer injuries and over 2 million are believed to suffer from ill health caused by work.

This is all estimated to cost the British economy up to £36 billion a year. Here are some key features of this waste:

- the most common forms of work-related ill health are back problems and other aches and pains, affecting 1.1 million people every year and costing the loss of 11.8 million working days
- about half a million people say they suffer work-related stress at a level that makes them ill
- 25,000 people are forced to give up work for good every year because of injuries or ill health caused at work.

This pattern is repeated to a greater or lesser extent across Europe, and therefore the European Union has recognised its responsibilities and established a European Agency for Safety and Health at Work at Bilbao to collect and analyse data, disseminate information and promote research and publicity. For a number of years now, the European Commission has promoted a European Week of Health and Safety at Work, organised by the European Agency.

In Britain a number of competitions are organised around this event and the razzmatazz that they bring to a subject too often regarded as tedious and technical is worthwhile. Entering a competition is a fairly cost-free, less formal method of benchmarking performance and bringing some transparency to your company's performance. Being in a competition can motivate managers and the workforce and, whether or not the company wins an award, participation can bring welcome positive local or national publicity, particularly if the local community has been involved.

A number of trade federations also promote awards for health and safety achievement for their sectors, and campaigning organisations such as RoSPA and the British Safety Council run events of their own. Participation in events such as these sends a very positive message to the workforce about the management's commitment and can enhance a company's reputation among competitors, customers and suppliers. It is also worth a director asking why his company plays no part in such awards if this is the case. It may be a symptom of something much more serious. In any case, an in-house awards scheme might be a good introduction and enable management to assess the value of joining a wider competition. It would also be another mechanism for ensuring that health and safety continues to play a proper and vibrant part in the life of the company.

Keeping up this momentum has a very particular practical consequence. The new attitude of the HSE is to reduce the number of inspections but to increase their depth and severity. A well-run business can therefore expect to avoid a visit. On the other hand, poor performance may invite attention. In the past, many companies would simply wait for a visit by an inspector to be told where they were going wrong, and would then fix the matters raised by the inspector. This passive approach did nothing to improve overall health and safety.

Today, the chances of being selected for an inspection by the enforcement authority depend on a number of factors and are not as high for some as they used to be. The HSE has recently been concentrating on certain high hazard sectors of industry (construction, agriculture and health services) and on five priority topics (falls from height, workplace transport, slips and trips, musculoskeletal disorders and stress). To these has been added the government's own performance as an exemplar. As a result, the HSE plans far fewer inspections than it undertook a decade or so ago, but these will be in-depth examinations of how a company is handling a specific hazard like stress or musculoskeletal disorders. If a company has been targeted for inspection, it probably means that the regulator regards it as a high risk business, is concerned about the incidence of injury or ill health, or is generally not very impressed by its management of health and safety.

Don't wait for the inspector to call. You are less likely to attract unwelcome regulatory attention if your company's reputation for managing health and safety is good. A self-sufficient approach that follows the lines outlined in the previous chapters, based on policy, planning and implementation, monitoring, audit and review, is recognised and respected by the enforcing authorities, as is the active involvement of the workforce and safety representatives.

Action

Directors will want to:

- walk around the workplace, talk to people about their work, ask 'idiot' questions like 'why do you do it this way?' and give encouragement. People are generally pleased to talk about their work and can give insights into working practices, and often have useful suggestions to make. That is why successful companies like Jaguar Cars positively encourage workers to make recommendations for improving health and safety. They find that these suggestions often also result in improved productivity
- try to 'catch' people doing things right and praise their behaviour
- encourage workers to voice their health and safety concerns and ensure that they are addressed – it's vital to build trust.

References and further reading

Reason, J. *Achieving a safe culture: theory and practice* (*Work and Stress*, vol. 12 no. 3, 1998, pp. 293–306)

HSE. *Director leadership – case studies*
(www.hse.gov.uk/corporateresponsibility/casestudies)

HSE. *Health and safety climate survey tool*, Misc 097 (HSE Books, Sudbury, 1997)

HSE. *Successful health and safety management*, HSG65 (HSE Books, Sudbury, 2003)

HSE. *Reducing error and influencing behaviour*, HSG48 (HSE Books, Sudbury 1999)

HSE and the Institute of Directors, free leaflet. *Leading health and safety at work*, INDG417 (HSE Books, Sudbury, 2007)

Institution of Occupational Safety and Health, free document. *Behavioural safety: kicking bad habits* (IOSH, Leicester, 2006)

Institution of Occupational Safety and Health, free document. *Promoting a positive culture – a guide to health and safety culture* (IOSH, Leicester, 2004)

Chapter 13
Managing risks to the environment

"Development that meets the needs of the present without compromising the ability of future generations to meet their own needs." Brundtland Commission's definition of sustainable development, 1987

So far we have been concerned primarily with what goes on in and around the workplace. By both law and custom, that is how we tend to think about health and safety. It is part of our history, in which employers gradually recognised their direct responsibility for the people they employed in their workplaces. It is what, from the Factories Acts onward, Parliament has reinforced and codified, gradually extending the scope until it recognised management's much wider responsibility for the good health of employees.

Yet, this definition of a company's impact has increasingly been seen as too restricted. How a business conducts itself affects the community much more widely. Its decisions do not concern only its shareholders and employees but also affect large numbers of people outside. Through its procurement practices it sets standards and demands action by other companies. Its products affect the wholesale and retail supply chain. They use resources and energy in their manufacture and distribution, and often in their ultimate use. Whatever is made or sold wears out and needs disposal. Its components may be toxic and can endanger people and pollute and damage the earth. A company's selling methods, advertising and public relations can change lifestyles and encourage bad habits as well as good.

It is for all these reasons that the citizen no longer thinks that companies have responsibility only for themselves, their shareholders, and their employees. Instead, they are expected to recognise much wider responsibilities to the community at large and, even beyond that, to the planet itself. The 'stakeholders' in a big and successful business are thus drawn from an ever wider circle of interests whose expectations are increasingly demanding. Collectively, from campaigning lobby groups to shareholder activists, such stakeholders help to define the context in which companies now do business. Some people even refer to this as a business's 'licence to operate'. And, in considering the right to that licence, concern for companies' impact on the environment has risen up most stakeholders' agendas.

Earlier (Chapter 3) we said that safety, health, and environment is not meant to be a series of rules but a culture within which a business learns to work in a safe, healthy and environmentally friendly way. As with other issues, therefore, in managing their environmental risks companies have both to comply with the requirements of the law and to measure up to the wider expectations of society.

Satisfying the law

There is now a substantial body of environmental laws that lay direct duties on businesses. Those that fail to comply risk prosecution and even the imprisonment of their directors. Nonetheless, the real issue for many is the serious reputational damage that such pronounced failure would entail. These issues make demands well beyond mere compliance and directors are becoming more aware of the true cost of poor environmental management.

Put positively, a well-founded and well-executed environmental policy will enable a company to avoid costs that regulation and reputational damage would otherwise impose. It will enable significant savings that go straight to the bottom line and it will meet the increasing expectations of the investment community, customers and shareholders.

So, the first responsibility of the director is to ensure that his business is not incurring serious risk because it has not got an adequate environmental policy in place. Compliance with the law is only the first step in such a programme and is, after all, only what would be expected of even the least capable of companies. Nonetheless, let us first deal with those specific legal requirements.

Policy principles – the EU dimension

The legal framework plays an important but not exclusive part in environmental protection. The European Union lays down the principles within which the countries of Europe develop their environmental policies and legislation. These issues are bound to cross borders: air and water pollution do not respect national frontiers. The Single Market means that a level playing field in environmental requirements is important for fair competition. Indeed, manufacturers and providers of services are best able to make environmental improvements if the regulatory regime covers a significant market area and is clear in its demands.

The key principles underlying EU policy to protect the environment are:

- the precautionary principle, which demands that we act with due care, forethought and research, and weigh the advantages of any action against the risk
- producer responsibility, which demands that we take responsibility for whatever we put on the market, including its disposal
- the polluter pays principle, which lays the liability for the communal, external environment costs of commercial and industrial activities on the shoulders of those who have caused the problem
- sustainable development, which requires that we should grow in a way that neither damages the world of today nor diminishes the resources that our children will inherit.

These principles mean that companies must, at the very least, follow two guiding concepts:

- the 'best available techniques' (BAT) are to be used
- the 'best practicable environmental option' (BPEO) is to be chosen.

There is a comprehensive directive on Integrated Pollution Prevention and Control (IPPC) (96/61/EC), which lays down measures designed to prevent or, where that is not practicable, reduce emissions to air, land and water. EU member states must implement IPPC by October 2007. However, EU environmental law goes much further than this, particularly in enforcing the principles of producer responsibility. This started in 1994 with its packaging waste policy and has been extended more recently with the publication of two producer responsibility directives designed to deal with two other waste streams – Waste Electrical and Electronic Equipment (WEEE) and End of Life Vehicles (ELV). The WEEE Directive aims to minimise the impact on the environment of the life cycle of a huge range of electrical and electronic equipment. The directive sets criteria for collection, treatment, recycling and recovery of waste electrical and electronic equipment and makes producers responsible for financing most of these activities. Householders are to be able to return waste equipment without charge. A secondary directive on the Restriction of Hazardous Substances complements the Waste Electrical and Electronic Equipment Directive by banning equipment containing more than agreed levels of hazardous substances such as lead, cadmium or mercury. The End of Life Vehicles Directive is very similar, restricting the use of certain heavy metals in vehicle manufacture, and ensuring that, from 2006, a large percentage of each vehicle is reused, recovered or recycled. The Batteries Directive (2006/66/EC) extends producer responsibility to the safe disposal of batteries. Member states have until September 2008 to transpose its requirements into domestic law.

Environmental protection law in the UK

Before this EU framework, there was a long history of law aimed at controlling pollution in the UK. Indeed, the British experience has been an important influence in the creation of European law. Maintaining air and water quality was a concern of government even before the pioneering reforms of the nineteenth and twentieth centuries, when the Alkali Acts of 1863 and 1906 were passed to control harmful emissions from 'smoke stack' industries. Disraeli's Public Health Acts did much to improve water quality and later governments continued to legislate through such mould-breaking laws as the Town and Country Planning Act 1947, the Clean Air Act 1963, and the Wildlife and Countryside Act 1981.

However, this was all piecemeal legislation covering specific risks to land, air and water, and it evolved over decades. It was not until 1990 that this whole range of issues was brought together by the Environmental Protection Act, followed in 1995 by the amalgamation of most of the key regulators (Her Majesty's Inspectorate of Pollution, the National Rivers Authority, Pollution Control Boards) into the Environment Agency.

Since then, responsibilities for the environment have been devolved by Westminster to the Scottish Parliament and Welsh Assembly but the approach across the UK, including Northern Ireland, is broadly similar. Underpinned by a statutory duty of care, there are strict controls over:

- atmospheric emissions, by conditions in licences and permits
- effluent discharges, by licences and permits
- contained, controlled waste (ie commercial, industrial, household or any such waste), by a duty of care and a code of practice on handling, storage,

treatment, transport and disposal of controlled waste, with conditions set in waste management licences

- hazardous waste, by classification and controls over containment, handling, transfer and disposal
- packaging, by design and labelling, recovery and recycling obligations.

The principal statutes dealing with the environment are listed in Part 3. Numerous regulations have been made under these and more legislation is on its way. The government's new five-year plan for the environment, 'Delivering the essentials of life', sets out plans which centre on:

- providing cleaner, greener, safer and healthier local environments through the Clean Neighbourhoods and Environment Act 2005 which will provide powers to deal with nuisances such as fly-tipping and litter
- changing the behaviour of government, business, farming and consumers to help reduce impacts on the environment and improve sustainability. The government promises to set up a Business Resource Efficiency and Waste Programme to help businesses with their environmental impacts
- improving energy efficiency – not least because climate change was high on the agenda for Britain's presidencies of the G8 and the EU in 2005.

Meeting wider expectations

Regulatory requirements are, of course, not the only reasons for a company to try to reduce its environmental impact. Public opinion, too, is an increasingly powerful driver for action to protect the environment. The Brent Spar saga was a bruising public relations experience for Shell, in spite of the fact that the company may well have been right about the environmental advantages of its preferred method of disposal. Serious damage to the company's reputation was done by the intervention of Greenpeace and the torrent of adverse publicity. Despite company, scientific, and government reassurances, the public did not feel that it was right to use the seas in this way. For Shell, what had been considered merely a technical issue became a major reputational concern.

The growing interest of the public in these issues has meant that the international community has had to consider how to deal with concerns that go far beyond national boundaries. Even a trading group as large as the EU cannot operate in these areas without taking wider considerations into account. That is why international policies are being developed, particularly in response to concerns about sustainability and the effects of climate change.

The Rio Declaration

Alarm over the magnitude of the risks facing the earth's environment led to the 'Earth Summit', held in Rio de Janeiro in 1992. At the summit, 150 nations agreed to take action to:

- pursue sustainable development
- curb the risk of climate change by reducing emissions of carbon dioxide and other greenhouse gases
- protect the diversity of species and habitats (biodiversity)
- manage the conservation and sustainable development of the world's forests.

Sustainability

The UK's strategy for sustainable development sets out four processes to be pursued simultaneously if greater sustainability is to be achieved:

- social progress which meets everyone's needs
- effective protection of the environment
- prudent use of natural resources
- maintenance of high and stable levels of economic growth.

This strategy recognises that sustainable development is dependent not just on environmental but also economic and social performance. It also recognises that development is as necessary as sustainability. Change and growth are essential to humanity but must operate within sustainable parameters.

Sustainable development must, however, not be regarded simply as political idealism. Doing more with less has obvious business advantages and reducing consumption of resources can make very significant savings to a business's bottom line. Improving energy and water efficiency not only does good generally but can also make a particular contribution to a company's profits.

Climate change and the Kyoto Protocol

Most scientists agree that the Earth's climate is changing at a quickening pace, with potentially disastrous implications. The major cause is believed to be the growing pollution of the atmosphere with gases such as carbon dioxide and methane. Much of this pollution is man-made, the result of burning increasing amounts of fossil fuel since the Industrial Revolution. Increased levels of these 'greenhouse' gases trap more of the sun's radiation within the atmosphere and lead to higher temperatures, a process often known as the 'greenhouse effect'. The comparatively recent scientific understanding of this phenomenon means that using the atmosphere as a dumping ground is less and less acceptable as a waste management option. Littering the air with our debris is no more acceptable than littering our streets and parks, and is considerably more dangerous. Nonetheless, reducing greenhouse gas emissions globally is a colossal challenge, particularly given the rapidly increased burning of fossil fuels by developing countries.

In an attempt to begin the process of control, the Kyoto Protocol was launched in 1997. It was the first legally binding treaty aimed at cutting greenhouse gases and was ratified by Russia, the 55th signatory, in November 2004; it therefore covered enough of the world to come into effect in February 2005. There are now about 150 countries supporting the protocol.

Six greenhouse gases are targeted, of which carbon dioxide is seen as the most significant. Many industrial nations have committed themselves to a range of targets to reduce emissions of these gases by 2010. Recognising the problems faced by smaller and developing countries, some are allowed to increase their emissions in a limited way, while other, more developed, countries face deeper cuts in order to compensate. The average reduction on the 1990 figures across developed countries is 5.2 per cent by 2010.

Measures being pursued to halt the growth in global warming and to move towards a 'low-carbon economy' now include:

- burning less fossil fuel, eg by using renewable energy sources and increasing energy efficiency
- carbon trading, a market-based approach to curbing emissions of carbon dioxide, in which companies and countries buy and sell credits based on whether they have increased or reduced emissions in relation to agreed targets
- granting 'carbon credits' for planting forests, initiating and using new

carbon-free technology, and other measures that directly benefit the battle against climate change

• planting 'carbon sink' forests to absorb carbon dioxide.

While the Kyoto Protocol is certainly a start, it will not solve the longer term problem. The Intergovernmental Panel on Climate Change suggested in a report in 1990 that a 60 per cent reduction in emissions was needed; cuts of two thirds of present emissions are now being talked about. These long term necessities will be difficult to achieve in any event and particularly so if other options, such as nuclear power generation, remain so controversial. Nevertheless, the UK government has adopted the target of reducing emissions by 60 per cent by 2050. The international debate about tackling climate change continued at Copenhagen in 2009.

Biodiversity

The Rio Summit produced the Convention on Biological Diversity. This committed signatories to develop national strategies for the protection and sustainable use of biodiversity or to adapt existing programmes for that purpose. In the UK, the government published its own strategy in 1994 – 'Biodiversity: the UK action plan' (Department of the Environment, 1994). This describes the UK's biological resources, outlines a detailed plan for their protection and includes 391 species action plans, 45 habitat action plans and 162 local biodiversity action plans. This is now managed by the UK Biodiversity Partnership.

Biodiversity issues affect numerous companies through the planning process, but in particular those in the extractive and utilities industries that have direct, potentially harmful, impacts on land and habitats. There has been a recent push from investors such as Insight Investment to press companies in these sorts of industries to improve their performance on biodiversity issues. Insight and the world conservation body IUCN are currently calling for companies to use 'biodiversity offsets' – conservation activities which are intended to compensate for unavoidable harm to biodiversity caused by development projects.

Forestry

The Rio Summit also produced a Statement of Forest Principles, the first global consensus on the management of the world's forests, which states that forests and their complex ecological processes are essential to economic development and the maintenance of all forms of life. This was not a convention. Some countries opposed such a structure, believing that it would conflict with their rights to use their natural resources to meet national policy objectives. Therefore the statement is not legally binding but an attempt to work towards a global consensus on the management, conservation and sustainable development of all types of forest. It was hoped that it would form the basis of further negotiations towards a binding agreement and set standards for the management of all types of forest in developed and developing countries alike. The UK government launched a sustainable forestry programme as a result. This statement and its ensuing strategies affect all users, importers and retailers of wood and wood products.

Enforcement

Even though some campaign groups in the UK believe, given the seriousness of the issues, that fines imposed by the courts for environmental offences are generally too low, failure to comply with environmental legislation can lead to heavy fines. Six or seven-figure penalties can be expected for the most serious offences. For example, a fine of £4 million, subsequently reduced on appeal, was imposed on the harbour authority at Milford Haven after a major pollution incident occurred in 1996 when the Sea Empress ran aground, spilling some 70,000 tonnes of oil.

The Environment Agency in England and Wales, the Scottish Environmental Pollution Agency (SEPA) in Scotland, and the Environment and Heritage Service in Northern Ireland are the principal regulatory bodies responsible for enforcing environmental protection legislation in the UK. Local authorities also have an important enforcement role, including the setting of local targets for waste and recycling with which businesses must comply.

The Environment Agency has its headquarters in Bristol and employs over 10,000 people, mainly based in seven regional offices in England and the Environment Agency Wales. They are largely employed in regulating major industries, carrying out day-to-day monitoring and clean-up operations locally, and in flood defence work.

The Agency's goal is for industry and businesses to come to value the assets of a rich and diverse natural environment, reap the benefits of sustainable business practices, improve competitiveness and secure trust in the wider community. It wants organisations and individuals to minimise the waste they produce, reuse and recycle materials more intensively and use energy and materials more efficiently. In addition it aims to reduce the emission of chemical pollutants into the air to below the level at which they can do significant harm. They believe, therefore, that businesses will need to make drastic cuts in their emissions of greenhouse gases.

How the Environment Agency plans to achieve its goals, and what the plans mean for business, is to be found in 'Making it happen', the agency's corporate strategy for 2002–07. A programme of actions aims to reduce pollution levels in areas of heavy industry by focusing on those with the greatest environmental impact, reducing water contamination and watercourse pollution, cleaning up contaminated land sites, reducing soil pollutants, targeting harmful chemical discharges and continuing to promote 'green business practices'. 'Targeted waste surveys' will be carried out and the agency intends to work with local authorities to reduce environmental crime and help cut greenhouse gases.

It is worth noting that, where a major hazard site falls under the Control of Major Accidents Hazards Regulations (COMAH), the HSE shares enforcement responsibility with the environment agencies as joint competent authorities. This is because these cover risks both to health and safety and the environment (see Chapter 14).

Developing a company policy for managing risks to the environment

Responsible companies have to chart a course in a competitive world. Naturally they will want to comply with existing law and environmental standards. A company will also want to act in a way that satisfies the expectations of its customers, investors and other stakeholders. They are increasingly demanding and a company needs to keep sufficiently ahead of expectations to be recognised as wholly responsible.

It is from this position that a business is least vulnerable. It will have moved beyond mere compliance to being well prepared for future legislation and regulation. It will have used the advantages inherent in sensible environmental management and control of waste, energy and water to avoid legal action and fines and, more positively, to reduce its overheads significantly. It will have found innovative ways to reduce its environmental impact and thus to save money and enhance its reputation.

All this derives from the use of standard business techniques. First, there is the need to identify the environmental impact the business creates and the risks posed to the company and the environment. Primary effects are most likely to stem from the use of resources (energy, water and so on) and the direct production of waste and emissions as a result. For example, a primary effect such as a serious spillage of controlled waste (say, a toxic chemical) is likely to have a significant impact capable of contaminating land or polluting water, killing fish or affecting the public drinking supplies. All of these primary effects are subject to legal controls with which companies must comply.

Again, in terms of waste management, most businesses, even purely service industries, produce waste of some kind that has to be disposed of in an environmentally acceptable manner. Some of it may be classified as 'hazardous waste'. Its disposal can be an expensive headache for the responsible company, for whom illegal dumping is not an option. Most hazardous waste generated in Britain is sent for disposal in licensed landfill sites (where it attracts landfill tax) or for controlled incineration. However, these options may change as environmental controls are tightened throughout Europe.

Businesses also have secondary impacts, which are more remote but even more pervasive than primary impacts. These include those effects incurred through the supply chain and in the life cycle of the product being sold. They are very often crucially important for a company's reputation.

Therefore, just like risks to health and safety, risks to the environment from a company's activities need to be assessed, monitored and managed. The vocabulary used by environmental experts is a little different but the principles of management are much the same – except that, because the scope of environmental responsibility is so much wider, the reliance on specific and particular standard measures is less appropriate. For that reason, although international standards are useful in creating effective environmental management systems, they must not be seen as the be-all and end-all of meeting a company's environmental responsibilities. Just as the creation of a climate of working safely and healthily is so important, so too a company must own its environmental policy in such a way that it informs every decision it makes.

Even so, measurement is the key. Vague statements are soon seen as the 'greenwash' they are. It is only when a company has an effective management system that enables impacts such as energy, water and waste to be measured and controlled that it can properly be said to meet today's expectations.

Standards

It is therefore in that spirit that a company should approach the key international standards for managing environmental risks.

ISO 14001

The International Organization for Standardization's environmental standard, ISO 14001:2004, is a useful guide to developing a company's policy for environmental management. The policy should:

- be defined by top management
- be appropriate to the nature, scale and environmental impacts of the organisation's activities, products and services
- include a commitment to compliance with relevant environmental legislation and regulations, and other requirements to which the organisation subscribes (eg the Chemical Industry Association's Responsible Care programme)

- include a commitment to continual improvement and prevention of pollution
- provide the framework for setting and reviewing environmental objectives and targets
- be documented, implemented and maintained, and communicated to employees
- be available to the public.

Just as for health and safety, it is good practice for the policy to be signed by the chief executive or another senior director.

ISO 14001 also sets out a specification for an environmental management system (EMS). Steps to be taken are:

- making a commitment to continual improvement and establishing a baseline of environmental impacts (for each site in question; ISO 14001 works on a site by site basis)
- identifying and ensuring compliance with legal and other requirements
- developing objectives, targets and programmes to monitor and manage impacts
- documentation, implementation and operation of the EMS
- checking, audit and review
- gaining acknowledgement of the EMS, eg by certification to ISO 14001 or registration to the EU's Eco-Management and Audit Scheme (EMAS – see below).

Like the approach to devising a health and safety management system, an EMS conforming to international standards is built on the key steps of 'plan, do, check, act'. This may provide an effective basis for meeting a company's environmental responsibilities. However, it is only a beginning. A greater degree of involvement and imagination will be necessary if a company is going to produce a policy and management system that are likely to prepare it for future regulation, ensure that it reduces present costs, and provide opportunity for using environmental performance to enhance its reputation and find ways of saving by growing in a sustainable way.

Management needs to be fully involved in working out a programme that makes environmental considerations work for company profitability instead of being seen as a box-ticking exercise that is an obstacle to enterprise. Instead, companies need a programme that will meet society's demands in a way that is cost effective and indeed profitable.

EMAS

EMAS (the EU's Eco-Management and Audit Scheme) is another management tool which allows European companies and other organisations to evaluate, report and improve their environmental performance. Like ISO 14001 it is a voluntary scheme that aims to recognise and reward those organisations that go beyond minimum legal compliance and continuously improve their environmental performance. The scheme also requires participating organisations to produce a regular public environmental statement that reports on their environmental performance. For this reason, EMAS is less popular with companies than ISO 14001. The Institute of Environmental Management and Assessment offers advice on implementing this process (see References).

Key environmental performance indicators

What gets measured gets done. It is the board's role to set objectives and targets. An environmental policy needs to cover a wide range of issues, but not everything can be done at once. This is why it is important to concentrate on some realistic key performance indicators (KPIs) that will ensure measurement of the basics in order to try to reduce these impacts. Over time it is important to develop a programme to add other KPIs at a pace that the business can properly accommodate.

KPIs need to be agreed by the board and communicated to the workforce as well as managers and supervisors if real progress is to be made towards the targets. The principle is the same as that already discussed for health and safety. KPIs should be SMART (specific, measurable, agreed, realistic and timescaled).

For operational performance these should as a minimum include the measurement of:

- energy used
- water used
- carbon emitted
- waste produced and methods of disposal/recycling
- substances released as emissions or effluent
- spillage incidents.

The data should be measured and presented in totals (absolute) and per unit of production (relative), eg per unit of space, per employee or per unit of revenue.

Indicators of management performance might include a series of assessments that have value in their own right, such as:

The management of risk

- risk assessments completed
- audits conducted
- employees trained

The management of the supply chain

- suppliers audited
- contractors inducted

The management of compliance

- complaints received, eg about noise, nuisance
- regulatory actions against non-compliance
- fines paid

The management of staff

- employee consultation on staff attitudes (towards the environmental policy)
- staff training programmes assessed

The management of community relationships

- community impact assessed
- engagement system established
- policy established for community support
- customer surveys conducted.

It is important that these matters should be covered but in a manner and according to a timetable that is reasonable. A monitoring system will be needed to measure performance. The board should expect to receive regular progress reports and to set challenging but achievable targets for improvement.

External guidance

There is, of course, plenty of official guidance available. For example, detailed advice on issues such as the necessary permits and licences for storing and disposing of hazardous waste is to be found on the Environment Agency's website (see References). The agency also publishes a quarterly magazine, *Your Environment*, which contains news about developments in environmental policy and numerous environmental reports, technical and scientific reports and information leaflets, some of them priced and others free to download from its website. A free website called Netregs (www.environment-agency.gov.uk/netregs) has been opened by the environment agencies to help small businesses. The Department for Environment, Food and Rural Affairs (DEFRA) publishes guidance on greenhouse gases, waste and water. Information is also available from sources such as Business in the Community and the EU (see References).

The most successful external guidance is that which will enable a company to implement an environmental strategy that will be cost-effective, avoid fines and the expense of unbudgeted regulatory demands, and improve the bottom line. In this, professional external help can be particularly valuable. Effective consultants should not only have a clear view of what is needed to comply with the law; they should also be able to help a company use environmental policy change to reduce its costs and environmental impacts. Above all, they should have an expert understanding of the way things are developing in the UK, the EU and the wider world. They will then be best placed to advise how a company can make changes in the normal course of business so that it is prepared for regulatory or legislative demands and does not have to face unnecessary expense. It is important that such advice is given at board level, to create an understanding of the wider implications of the decisions that have to be made.

Disclosure and reporting

Just as with health and safety, companies need to respond to the growing pressure for public reporting of their performance in environmental management. The systems of risk assessment and data collection need to be fully capable of producing solid and rigorous figures which will stand up to the scrutiny of outside commentators. Yet, even without publication, these are precisely the kind of figures necessary to enable the effective setting of a baseline against which future performance and targets can be measured.

For many companies environmental reporting has been subsumed into wider non-financial reporting, often as part of a corporate social responsibility report. Although not compulsory, this is an increasingly favoured way among FTSE 100 and FTSE 350 companies of responding to the wider expectations of society and stakeholders. While corporate social responsibility and sustainability reports vary, the sort of ground which needs to be covered is widely agreed and set out in the sustainability reporting guidelines published in 2002 by the Global Reporting Initiative (GRI – see References). The initiative has managed since 1997 to engage thousands of stakeholders with interests in reporting – from business, accountancy bodies and trade unions to investor organisations and NGOs – and has subsequently put together a set of reporting guidelines which have achieved worldwide acceptance. These guidelines are increasingly seen by investors and others as the standard for public disclosure of environmental impacts, performance data and targets.

Further impetus has come in the form of the DTI's rules for the Operating and Financial Review (OFR). These came into effect in 2005 and require quoted companies to report on their performance in January 2006 and annually thereafter (see also Chapter 11).

Action

Directors will need to know whether the company has a strategy for environmental risk management and, in particular, they will want to be assured that the business has:

- assessed its environmental risks in a rigorous manner
- consulted inside and outside the company
- developed a policy statement as a result
- ensured that the policy has been discussed and approved by the board
- nominated a director responsible for implementing the policy
- fixed mechanisms for measuring performance
- established KPIs
- set targets for improvement
- considered certification to ISO 14001 or registration with EMAS
- made sure that the board receives and discusses reports
- set a timetable for reporting publicly
- challenged the board to think strategically about reducing the company's environmental impact.

References and further reading

British Standards Institution. *BS 8555:2003 Environmental management systems – guide to the phased implementation of an environmental management system including the use of environmental performance evaluation* (BSI Publications, London, 2003)

British Standards Institution. *BS EN ISO 14001:2004 Environmental management systems. Requirements with guidelines for use* (BSI Publications, London, 2004)

Business in the Community. *Business in the environment* (www.bitc.org.uk/programmes/programme_directory/business_in_the_environment)

Control of Major Accident Hazards Regulations 1999, SI 1999/743 (HMSO, London)

Council of the European Union. Council Directive 96/61/EC of 24 September 1996 concerning integrated pollution prevention and control. (*Official Journal* L257, 10 October 1996, pp. 26–40)

Department for Environment, Food and Rural Affairs website, www.defra.gov.uk

Department for Environment, Food and Rural Affairs. *General guidelines on environmental reporting* (www.defra.gov.uk/environment/envrp/general/index.htm)

Directorate-General for Employment and Social Affairs. *Promoting a European framework for corporate social responsibility* (Green Paper, European Commission, Brussels, 2001)

Environment Agency website, www.environment-agency.gov.uk

Environmental Protection Act 1990, ch 43 (HMSO, London)

European Commission. *EMAS – the Eco-management and Audit Scheme* website, www.europa.eu.int/comm/environment/emas/tools/faq_en.htm

European Union. *Activities of the European Union: Environment* website, www.europa.eu.int/pol/env/index_en.htm

Global Reporting Initiative website, www.globalreporting.org

Hyde, P, and Reeve, P. *Essentials of environmental management* (IOSH Services, Leicester, 2004)

Institute of Environmental Management and Assessment website, www.iema.net

Institution of Occupational Safety and Health, free document. *Making a difference – a basic guide to environmental management for OSH practitioners* (IOSH, Leicester, 2009)

Intergovernmental Panel on Climate Change, www.ipcc.ch

Scottish Environmental Protection Agency website, www.sepa.org.uk

United Nations. *The Earth Summit 1992: Rio Declaration on environment and development* (Rio de Janeiro, 3–14 June 1992)

United Nations. *Kyoto Protocol to the United Nations Framework Convention on climate change, Kyoto, 11 December 1997* (United Nations, New York, 1997)

Chapter 14
Major hazards

"…the safety case enables those who carry on a particular activity to demonstrate that they have systematically identified the hazards, assessed the risks and put into effect measures for eliminating them or reducing them to an acceptable level."
The Rt Hon Lord Cullen

Major hazards are subject to both safety and planning controls. The aim is to prevent and mitigate the consequences of major accidents which can cause harm to people or the environment. This kind of event usually involves the large scale release of toxic or flammable substances. The risks of occurrence may be remote but the consequences are far reaching.

If your company has such risks to manage, be aware that you have to conform to very stringent rules and procedures, usually involving you in preparing a safety case and gaining its acceptance by regulatory authorities. The safety case will need to demonstrate that risks have been comprehensively assessed and that appropriate controls and management systems are in place for safe operation.

Directors will need to be aware of the regulatory controls over major hazards, and in particular the Control of Major Accident Hazards (COMAH) Regulations, which are discussed below. Directors also need to heed the approved code of practice and guidance published by the HSC in support of the Management of Health and Safety at Work Regulations 1999, which have been discussed in Chapter 2.

The evolution of controls in the UK
In October 1966, 144 people, including 116 schoolchildren, died when a tip of coal waste slid down a hillside into the Welsh mining village of Aberfan and engulfed the junior school. As is often the case after a disaster, legislative action was then taken to control tips and prevent such a horrific event recurring.

But the expression 'major hazard' entered the UK's health and safety lexicon one Saturday morning in 1974, when a disaster occurred at a chemical works at Flixborough in Lincolnshire, killing 28 workers on site and damaging more than

2,000 houses and other premises around the plant. A massive explosion of highly flammable materials being processed at high temperature and pressure had occurred when a temporary bypass in pipework failed catastrophically.

After Aberfan, Flixborough was the worst industrial accident to occur in the UK until the Piper Alpha fire in 1988. Inventories of hazardous materials both in storage and process at chemical works and refineries had been growing for some years. The risks were feared but not well understood. Flixborough was a 'wake-up call' about the serious risks to the public as well as to workers from large-scale industrial activities.

Public inquiries, followed by legislation to implement recommendations, are the normal political response to catastrophe in the UK. After Flixborough, an inquiry was held, recommendations were published and an advisory committee was established by the newly formed HSC. But progress thereafter was slow in agreeing appropriate regulatory controls for what began to be known as 'major hazards'.

The tolerability of risk

During the 1980s a series of public inquiries into new nuclear power stations helped refine the thinking further, particularly the inquiry into a proposed pressurised water reactor at Sizewell in Suffolk. The inspector holding the inquiry, Sir Frank Layfield, asked the Nuclear Installations Inspectorate to define the 'tolerability of risk' (an expression later colloquially called 'TOR').

TOR was subsequently defined by the HSE in its publication *The tolerability of risk from nuclear plants*. Nuclear safety continues to be regulated according to the principles it explains, but these principles run wider than the nuclear industry and have informed regulation of other major industrial hazards based on reducing risks 'as low as reasonably practicable', known as the 'ALARP principle'. This approach has won widespread support from the industries concerned.

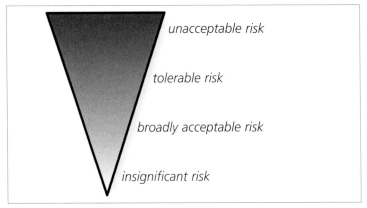

unacceptable risk

tolerable risk

broadly acceptable risk

insignificant risk

The basic TOR diagram

Essentially, TOR describes risk in a way which grades it from unacceptable through tolerable to acceptable, and explains this process in relation to reducing risks 'as low as reasonably practicable', in full compliance with the philosophy of the Health and Safety at Work etc Act 1974, which as we have already seen requires health and safety to be ensured 'so far as is reasonably practicable'. The area of 'tolerability' equates to what is believed 'safe enough'.

Reducing risks, protecting people

Risk gives rise to a great deal of discussion and hot air today. What exactly is meant by an intolerable risk? Even in Victorian times the concept was well understood. The use of yellow phosphorus was banned in the manufacture of matches after public outrage at the incidence of 'phossy jaw' among the East End match girls. More recently, lead glazes were banned in pottery manufacture because of the risk of poisoning, and it is illegal to employ young persons under 18 years old in any work activities where there is a risk of exposure to high lead levels. Other substances were banned in the 1960s after they were found to have carcinogenic effects. These are the sorts of risk that British society has judged 'intolerable' and to which the regulators have had to respond.

After further consultations with industry in 1999, the HSE set out the general framework for its decision making processes, exercised under its authority as the national regulator of health and safety at work, in its publication *Reducing risks, protecting people* (2001). Colloquially known as 'R2P2', this is a valiant attempt to show that the decision making process can have consistency and coherence across the whole spectrum of risks, including those from major hazards, which fall within the scope of the Health and Safety at Work etc Act 1974.

Essentially, the framework sees risk categorised as unacceptable, tolerable or broadly acceptable. Levels of risk are categorised according to the potential harm to the individual and societal concerns which accompany it. Control measures are implemented to reduce risks to ALARP, which does not necessarily mean achieving zero risk. The harmful consequences of any accident are mitigated by further control measures.

Good practice is described as the consensus as to what constitutes proportionate action to control a given hazard, taking account of what is technically feasible, the balance of costs and benefits and, if necessary, other relevant factors. This regulatory philosophy is based on the risk of death to an individual being broadly acceptable if calculated at one in 1 million per annum. The risk is intolerable at one in 1,000 for workers and one in 10,000 for members of the public.

Nuclear

The nuclear power generation and fuel reprocessing industries were among the first to be subjected to 'major hazard' controls. After the UK's worst nuclear accident, at Windscale (now Sellafield) in 1957, when a pile (or reactor) caught fire and released radioactive material, the Nuclear Installations Act was introduced. This established the Nuclear Installations Inspectorate (NII, now part of the HSE) and brought into effect a licensing regime.

The NII's safety assessment principles, or SAPs, were later published so that nuclear operators would know where the goalposts stood when seeking a licence.

The NII expects the operator to make out a satisfactory case for operating safely (the 'safety case') with risks reduced as low as reasonably practicable before granting them a licence, which will contain conditions. The NII will inspect the operation with reference to conditions imposed by the licence.

The ultimate enforcement sanction against nuclear operators is the NII's right to revoke their licence to operate if they have concerns about unsafe operation.

Offshore oil and gas

Regulation of major hazard industries has tended to be by sector, pursuing parallel but distinct tracks, depending on the accident history. In the North Sea oil and gas industry, for example, the worst ever accident occurred on the Piper Alpha installation in 1988. Fires and explosions claimed the lives of 167 people and the installation was destroyed after a failure in maintenance procedures. Lord Cullen chaired the public inquiry and his groundbreaking report made a number of significant recommendations.

One was that regulation of the offshore oil and gas industry should be transferred from the industry's sponsor department, the then Department of Energy, to the HSE. This established the important principle that it was essential to safety that responsibility for economic sponsorship should be kept separate from responsibility for enforcement of safety regulations, and that the safety regulator should be independent. Lord Cullen further recommended that designers and operators of oil and gas installations should make out a case for safety and submit it to the regulator for acceptance. A decade later, this approach appeared to have been highly successful with no further major accidents in the North Sea.

Railways

Responsibility for railway safety was similarly transferred to the HSE from the Department of Transport, the sponsoring department for railways, after several disasters such as the Clapham collision and the King's Cross underground station fire had occurred. A safety case regime was then introduced for Britain's railways during the privatisation of British Railways in the 1990s, based on the concept of the regulator accepting (or not) a safety case from an 'infrastructure controller' responsible for the lines, signalling and stations, which in turn accepted (or not) safety cases from train operators.

The recent train crashes on Britain's railways at Southall, Paddington, Hatfield and Potters Bar raised serious questions about the robustness of the regulatory regime. Lord Cullen's public inquiry into the Paddington collision endorsed the safety case approach but ministers have since listened to representations from the industry that too many parties were involved in its regulation, and have decided to transfer the Railway Inspectorate from the HSE to the economic regulator.

Gas

There have been several serious accidents following the rupture of gas mains, of which until a few years ago many thousands of kilometres were the original

Victorian cast iron mains laid a century or more ago. These are steadily being replaced by plastic pipes, thought likely to have at least similar durability.

Regulations to control the safety of Britain's gas distribution system introduced a safety case regime for gas transmission based on the concept of an infrastructure or 'network' controller and the acceptance of safety cases by the regulator, the HSE.

Explosives

The explosives industry is one of the earliest to have been regulated by a major hazards control regime. The manufacture, use and storage of explosives has been subject to licensing since Victorian times. The requirements of the Explosives Act were recently substantially revised and updated by the Manufacture and Storage of Explosives Regulations 2005 and an Approved Code of Practice.

Regulations made in 1983 require the classification and labelling of explosives according to UN standards.

Control of Major Accident Hazards Regulations (COMAH)

We have seen above how several industrial sectors with the potential for major accidents have become the subject of customised safety case regimes. The majority of the 1,000 or so chemical plants and similar manufacturing or storage sites with major hazards in the UK are subject to yet another safety case regime, this time laid down by the European Commission.

Initially, following Flixborough, the Notification of Industrial Hazardous Sites Regulations and the Control of Industrial Major Accident Hazard Regulations were made to deal with these kinds of risk in Great Britain. However, the

European Commission's so-called 'Seveso Directives', named after an environmental disaster involving the release of dioxins at Seveso in Italy, soon required more to be done by operators of these sites.

The Seveso II Directive (96/82/EC) was implemented in Britain by the Control of Major Accident Hazards (COMAH) Regulations. Regulation 4 requires operators of major hazard establishments to 'take all measures necessary to prevent major accidents and limit their consequences to persons and the environment'. This is consistent with the general duty in British health and safety law to reduce risks to a level that is as low as reasonably practicable. Generally, the aim is to ensure that the risk to an individual living near a site of being killed is less than one in a million per year.

Operators within scope are in two groups: those with 'lower-tier sites' and those with 'top-tier sites', depending on types and sizes of inventories.

'Lower-tier' operators are required to:

- notify certain details to the competent authority
- take all measures necessary to prevent major accidents and limit their consequences to people and the environment
- prepare a major accident prevention policy (MAPP).

'Top-tier' operators are not required to prepare a separate MAPP but must instead prepare a 'safety report'. This must include:

- a policy on how to prevent and mitigate major accidents
- a management system for implementing that policy

- an effective method for identifying any major accident risks
- measures to prevent and mitigate major accidents (such as safe plant and safe operating procedures)
- information on safety precautions built into the plant when it was designed and constructed
- details of measures (such as firefighting) to limit the consequences of any major accident
- information about the emergency plan for the site.

They must also:

- update the safety report every five years or after significant changes or new knowledge about safety matters
- prepare and test an on-site emergency plan
- supply information to local authorities for off-site emergency planning purposes
- provide certain information to the public about their activities.

Safety reports are made available to the public via public registers. The information about the emergency plan will be used by the local authority in drawing up an off-site emergency plan.

The COMAH Regulations cover risks to both people and the general environment and are therefore jointly enforced by the UK competent authorities, namely the Environment Agency, the Scottish Environmental Pollution Agency and the HSE. Memoranda of understanding have been agreed requiring co-operation between the authorities in the interests of consistent enforcement on businesses.

However, the ink had scarcely dried on these new regulations before the European Commission felt driven to tighten controls even further. While there had been no major disaster involving a British site since the fires at BP's Grangemouth oil refinery in 1987 and the fire at Hickson and Welch, Castleford, in 1992, catastrophes were continuing to occur elsewhere. A spill of hydrogen cyanide killed thousands of tonnes of fish in the River Tisza in Romania in 2000. Massive explosions at a fireworks factory at Enschede in the Netherlands killed 20 people and injured almost 1,000 more in 2000, devastating the surrounding area. In 2001 an explosion involving ammonium nitrate in a chemical works at Toulouse, France, killed 30 people.

Yet another EC Directive (2003/105/EC) has therefore followed, amending Seveso, and the COMAH Regulations have been updated with effect from 2005. The principles remain the same, but the amended Regulations are broader in scope, include certain new materials for the first time and amend the quantities and classifications of dangerous substances to which COMAH applies. Among other changes, the amendment also requires that schools, hospitals and other such establishments be provided with safety information and that specific training in planning for emergencies be given to all persons working in the establishment.

The purpose of all these regulations is to reduce risks and limit the consequences if things go wrong. Risk assessment should include consideration of the effects that organisational change may be having. Human factors, restructuring and consequent losses of corporate memory and experience have proved themselves a potent mix, contributing to the root causes of major incidents. Identification of the needs, competence and workloads of staff involved with safety-critical tasks is vital.

Risk assessment should also consider the consequences of an accident, by examining how staff are likely to react if things go wrong, looking at various scenarios and identifying training needs and any system weaknesses that may be exposed in a real emergency.

Action

A director of a business subject to major hazard controls will want to ensure that:

- the board is satisfied that the company is managing these risks properly
- the safety case/report is up to date and accepted by the regulator
- any outstanding issues with the regulators are being addressed
- risk assessments are up to date and valid
- the workforce is well trained in managing the risks
- emergency exercises are regularly conducted
- the company has good working relationships with the local emergency planning officer and the emergency services
- good communications have been established with the local community.

References and further reading

Control of Major Accident Hazard Regulations 1999, SI 1999/743 (HMSO, London)

Control of Major Accident Hazard (Amendment) Regulations 2005, SI 2005/1088 (HMSO, London)

Council of the European Communities. Council Directive 82/501/EEC of 24 June 1982 on the major accident hazards of certain industrial activities 'Seveso I' (*Official Journal of the European Communities* No. L230, 5 August 1982)

Council of the European Union. Council Directive 96/82/EC of 9 December 1997 on the control of major accident hazards involving dangerous substances 'Seveso II' (*Official Journal of the European Communities* No. L10/13, 14 January 1997)

Department of Employment. *The Flixborough disaster. Report of the Court of Inquiry* (HMSO, London, 1975)

Explosives Acts 1875 and 1923

Health and Safety at Work etc Act 1974, ch. 37 (HMSO, London)

HSE. *Management of health and safety at work. Management of Health and Safety at Work Regulations 1999 – Approved Code of Practice*, L21 (HSE Books, Sudbury, 2000)

HSE. *Organisational change and major accident hazards*, Chemical Information Sheet CHIS7 (HSE Books, Sudbury, 2003)

HSE. *Reducing risks, protecting people: HSE's decision-making process* (HSE Books, Sudbury, 2001)

HSE. *Safety assessment principles for nuclear plants* (HSE Books, Sudbury, 1992)

HSE. *The tolerability of risks from nuclear power stations* (HSE Books, Sudbury, 1988)

Hon. Lord Cullen. *The Public Inquiry into the Piper Alpha disaster*, Cm 1310 (HMSO, London, 1990)

Management of Health and Safety at Work Regulations 1999, SI 1999/3242 (HMSO, London)

Manufacture and Storage of Explosives Regulations 2005, SI 2005/1082 (HMSO, London)

Nuclear Installations Act 1965 (as amended 1969) (for Nuclear Licensed Sites) (HMSO, London)

Part 2
Hazards and controls A to Z

Introduction

Part 2 is in the form of a ready reference A to Z and aims to provide a busy director with basic information about the commoner hazards and risks, and some issues expected to rise in prominence in the near future.

Legal requirements, practical control measures and pointers towards good practice are briefly discussed. The A to Z is not intended to serve as a comprehensive legal or technical text, but should enable the non-expert to discuss risk issues with colleagues on the basis of at least some knowledge and understanding. More detailed advice should always be sought from in-house health and safety practitioners, from reputable consultants or from the regulatory authorities.

The general duties of the 1974 Act and the requirements of the Management of Health and Safety at Work Regulations 1999 will normally apply. In some instances other more specific regulations may also apply.

Absenteeism

Absenteeism is a term that can sound pejorative when applied to genuine sickness absence. There is no doubt, however, that this is a serious problem for management. According to CBI statistics, cases of long term sickness absence account for 33 per cent of lost working days, though only 5 per cent of all cases of absence. It is estimated to cost UK business around £3.8 billion a year.

'Presenteeism' is another term that is sometimes used in this context to describe the phenomenon of employees working when they should be at home because they are ill, or who work such long hours that they are no longer effective.

There are clear implications for productivity, profitability and workforce morale. Taking steps to tackle these problems will bring benefits such as retention of valued staff, a healthy workforce, improved workplace relations and reduction in overheads. See the discussion in Part 1 Chapter 12 on achieving a 'safety culture'.

References and further reading

HSE. *Managing sickness absence: a comprehensive guide for employers* (www.managingabsence.org.uk)

HSE. *Securing health together: a long-term occupational health strategy for England, Scotland and Wales* (HSE Books, Sudbury, 2000)

HSE. *Successful health and safety management*, HSG65 (HSE Books, Sudbury, 2003)

Agriculture

Farming is one of the most hazardous industries and has one of the worst industrial fatal accident incidence rates. Between 1994 and 2003, 483 people were killed in farming, forestry and horticulture activities. Thirty-eight people were killed in the sector in 2009/10. The statistics sadly include numerous children, often members of a farmer's family (see **Children**).

Accidents are commonly caused by transport, including overturning tractors or quad bikes without roll-over protection, contact with moving or unguarded machinery such as power take-off (PTO) shafts, drowning in slurry pits or grain silos, crushing by animals, electrocutions, falling from height such as from trees and through fragile roofs, and exposure to pesticides and other toxic chemicals.

Common ill health problems in this sector include musculoskeletal disorders, skin problems from exposure to chemicals, and certain infections caught from animals (see **Zoonoses**).

References and further reading

General duties, Health and Safety at Work etc Act 1974

Management of Health and Safety at Work Regulations 1999, SI 1999/3242
    (HMSO, London)

Alcohol

Alcohol is estimated to cause 8 to 14 million lost working days each year and
3 to 5 per cent of all absences from work in Great Britain. It is known to affect
judgment and co-ordination and increase risks of an accident, particularly in
safety-critical work. Short of that, it can reduce work performance, and a
drinking culture can give customers a bad impression of the company. In a survey
conducted in 1994, 90 per cent of personnel directors said that alcohol
consumption was a problem for their organisation.

The general duties of the 1974 Act and the risk assessment requirement of the
Management Regulations mean that employers have a duty to ensure the
health, safety and welfare of employees so far as is reasonably practicable.
Allowing employees to continue working if you know they are under the
influence of alcohol could expose them and others to risk, and would be in
breach of the law.

Under the Transport and Works Act 1992 it is a criminal offence for certain
workers to be unfit through drink or drugs while working on railways and similar
safety-critical transport systems, and operators must show all due diligence in
preventing an offence from being committed.

Companies are introducing policies for dealing with alcohol problems at work.
Advice from the HSE suggests that these should be based on four steps:

- find out if there is a problem
- if so, decide what to do about it
- take action
- check what you have done.

Detailed advice and case studies are contained in the HSE's free leaflet, *Don't mix it!*

Alcohol screening is adopted by some organisations, particularly those performing safety-critical tasks. It is a sensitive issue and only likely to succeed if the consent of the workforce is gained. Testing is costly and the results must be accurate if they are to be regarded as valid in disciplinary proceedings.

References and further reading

Department of Health. *Sensible drinking: the report of an interdepartmental working party* (DoH, 1996)

General duties, Health and Safety at Work etc Act 1974

Health Education Authority. *Attitudes towards alcohol in the workplace* (HEA, 1995)

HSE, free leaflet. *Don't mix it! A guide for employers on alcohol at work* (HSE Books, Sudbury, 1999)

Management of Health and Safety at Work Regulations 1999, SI 1999/3242 (HMSO, London)

Anthrax
See **Infections**.

Asbestos

Asbestos has killed more people in the UK over the last 100 years than any other occupational health hazard. The fibres of this naturally occurring mineral substance were identified as hazardous over a century ago but the first regulations controlling exposure to asbestos were not made until 1931. The law has been successively tightened as medical and scientific understanding of its dangers has grown.

Chrysotile (white), amosite (brown) and crocidolite (blue) asbestos have all been used in Britain in the past. The use of brown and blue asbestos has been banned in Britain for many years now and white asbestos has recently been banned by European Directive. While a few still argue that white asbestos, particularly in asbestos cement products, poses little risk, the courts will not excuse companies taking a chance with the health of their workforce or the public if they have to deal with any of these materials. Breaches of asbestos regulations are regarded by enforcing authorities as very serious. In recent years successful prosecutions have resulted in very heavy fines on companies and custodial sentences for directors and managers. Judges have disqualified some directors under the Companies Act.

Asbestos was used in Britain as a construction material very extensively from the 1950s to the mid-1980s. These days asbestos remains a serious risk to be managed, because for decades it was used widely as a fire protection material in building and plant construction, in lagging for insulation purposes and in products which may still be in use, particularly asbestos cement and insulation board. Drilling or cutting of materials containing asbestos will obviously create dust which could be inhaled. Processes causing major disturbance, such as demolition of buildings and removal of tiles, plaster and paint containing asbestos, are potentially very hazardous.

The HSE estimates that today there could be 500,000 non-domestic premises that contain asbestos materials, eg for fire protection, that could be disturbed during maintenance, demolition and other activities, exposing yet another generation of workers. Asbestos-related diseases are believed to have killed 50,000 people in the UK in the last 30 years and are currently still killing around 3,500 people a year.

Because of the long period of latency, something between 15 and 60 years, it can be many years after exposure before a person shows signs of suffering from an asbestos-related disease. Exposure does not have to be high or of long duration to cause disease. The diseases resulting from exposure to asbestos are all caused by inhalation of tiny, very fine asbestos fibres; they include asbestosis or fibrosis of the lungs, lung cancer and mesothelioma (cancer of the inner lining of the chest wall or abdominal cavity). There is no cure for any of these.

About a quarter of those dying are believed to have worked in the construction industry. Demolition workers, electricians, computer cabling installers, plumbers, decorators, building maintenance workers and the like are still at serious risk if asbestos is not managed properly. If a company or council is in the residential property rental business it should also be thinking about risks to residents.

Great care must therefore be taken to identify and control any asbestos hazards in a company's premises. There are control limits laid down for asbestos in air but these are not to be regarded as safe limits of exposure. Companies are required by law to reduce exposure to a level that is as low as is reasonably practicable.

Asbestos insulation may usually be safely left alone if it is in good condition and protected from damage so that fibres cannot be released. But sooner or later it will probably have to be dealt with. Some firms have opted to remove the hazard entirely, which itself can be a dangerous process. If it has not been done properly and left perfectly clean (the 'clearance' procedure) fibres will have been released into the atmosphere that could pose a serious threat to the health of workers or visitors returning to the building.

In other cases, contractors have been alleged to have exaggerated the size of the problem, causing unnecessary expense. Stripping and removal of asbestos should only be carried out by reputable specialist contractors. The HSE licenses such contractors.

Asbestos is one of the few hazardous substances not covered by the COSHH Regulations. Instead, it attracts specific regulations. Recently updated as the Control of Asbestos Regulations 2006, the law now contains a 'duty to manage', which requires those with responsibility for the repair and maintenance of non-domestic premises to find out whether there are or may be any materials containing asbestos. If so, the location and condition of the materials has to be recorded, the risk assessed and then managed. Information about the location and condition of asbestos-containing materials must be passed on to anyone liable to disturb them.

An approved code of practice gives guidance on how to comply with these regulations. It particularly emphasises the provision of suitable training and the importance of 'clearance' procedures (ie making sure that the area is left free of asbestos fibres) following work with asbestos.

An amendment to the European Asbestos Worker Directive requires a single control limit to be introduced for exposure to all forms of asbestos. Regulations are proposed to implement this in Great Britain by 15 April 2006. These will also simplify and consolidate existing regulations.

The HSE began a five-year campaign in 2001 to raise awareness of the risks from asbestos in buildings and the importance of the duty to manage the risk.

References and further reading

Control of Asbestos Regulations 2006, SI 2006/2739 (HMSO, London)

European Commission. Asbestos Worker Protection Directive 83/447/EEC (*Official Journal of the European Communities*, 18 August 1983)

HSE. *A comprehensive guide to managing asbestos in premises*, HSG227 (HSE Books, Sudbury, 2002)

HSE, free leaflet. *A short guide to managing asbestos in premises*, INDG223 (HSE Books, Sudbury, 2002)

HSE. *The management of asbestos in non-domestic premises. Regulation 4 of the Control of Asbestos at Work Regulations 2002 – Approved Code of Practice*, L127 (HSE Books, Sudbury, 2002)

HSE. *Work with materials containing asbestos. Control of Asbestos Regulations 2006. Approved Code of Practice and Guidance*, L143 (HSE Books, Sudbury, 2006)

HSE. *The management of asbestos in non-domestic premises, Regulation 4 of the Control of Asbestos Regulations 2006. Approved Code of Practice and guidance*, L127 (HSE Books, Sudbury, 2006)

Asthma

Occupational asthma can occur when workers inhale substances which cause a hypersensitive state in the airways, the passages carrying air to and from the lungs. If the lungs also become sensitised, even a low further exposure to the sensitiser involved may induce an asthma attack. Symptoms are coughing and wheezing, tightness in the chest or shortness of breath, rhinitis or conjunctivitis. Asthma is so disabling for some workers that they can never work again.

There are hundreds of known sensitising substances or asthmagens, including such diverse materials as isocyanates, dust, glutaraldehyde, the fumes of some solder fluxes, and storage mites. Substances known to be potential sensitisers should be identified by the risk phrase 'May cause sensitisation by inhalation' on labels or safety data sheets.

Some risk of asthma is likely to arise in most industrial sectors. The HSE estimates that 1,500 to 3,000 new cases of occupational asthma occur each year. The disease is believed to have cost society over £1 billion in the last decade.

The usual duties under health and safety law to protect the health of workers apply. The COSHH Regulations require risk assessments and control measures will include elimination of sensitising substances, substitution with something safer, enclosure in a contained process, local exhaust ventilation and personal protective equipment.

Different regulatory schemes apply to biocides and non-agricultural pesticides.

References and further reading

Asthma UK website, www.asthma.org.uk

Control of Substances Hazardous to Health Regulations 2002, SI 2002/2677
   (HMSO, London)

HSE, free leaflet. *Respiratory sensitisers and COSHH: Breathe freely – an employers' leaflet on preventing occupational asthma*, INDG95 (HSE Books, Sudbury, 1995)

Management of Health and Safety at Work Regulations 1999, SI 1999/3242 (HMSO, London)

Behavioural safety

See **Human factors**.

Biological agents

Biological agents include micro-organisms, cell cultures or human endoparasites, whether or not genetically modified, which may cause infection, allergy, poisoning or other hazards to human health. They are covered by the COSHH Regulations, which require risk assessment and prevention or control of exposure to any of these biological agents.

Other specific regulations also apply to:

- risks to human health and the environment associated with the use of genetically modified organisms (GMOs)
- legionella bacteria, which may occur in cooling towers and evaporative condensers in air conditioning systems
- anthrax
- transporting infectious micro-organisms.

See also **Genetically modified organisms, Infections.**

References and further reading

Carriage of Dangerous Goods and Use of Transportable Pressure Equipment
    Regulations 2004, SI 2004/568 (HMSO, London)

Control of Substances Hazardous to Health Regulations 2002, SI 2002/2677
    (HMSO, London)

Notification of Cooling Towers and Evaporative Condensers Regulations 1992,
    SI 1992/2225 (HMSO, London)

Bullying

Bullying at work is a more common phenomenon in companies than many managers recognise or care to admit. Some managers adopt bullying behaviour themselves to help them achieve the results for which they are accountable, yet they are unable to recognise that they are doing it.

The issue needs to be confronted and nipped in the bud before it causes stress and disruption. If not, it becomes a risk to the health and morale of workers and will cause damage to productivity and goodwill within the company. Cases are best dealt with by firm and fair application of the company's disciplinary procedures, with a clear declaration of intent from the board. Retraining may be appropriate.

See also **Violence**.

References and further reading

General duties, Health and Safety at Work etc Act 1974

Management of Health and Safety at Work Regulations 1999, SI 1999/3242
    (HMSO, London)

Chemicals

Thousands of different chemicals are used throughout industry and many are toxic, caustic, flammable or otherwise dangerous if stored or used improperly.

Suppliers of dangerous chemicals are required to comply with the Chemicals (Hazard Information and Packaging for Supply) Regulations, otherwise known as CHIP. CHIP aims to protect people and the environment from the effects of dangerous chemicals by requiring suppliers to provide information about them and package them safely.

Chemical suppliers and importers are also required under a European-wide system to obtain information about chemicals new to the European market that will help decide whether a chemical is dangerous. In Britain this system is implemented by the Notification of New Substances Regulations 1993 ('NONS') and administered by the HSE and the Environment Agency. The European Commission is also developing a new strategy, 'REACH', for the supply and control of chemicals throughout the EU, which is likely in due course to lead to further requirements.

Other regulations, such as COSHH, also apply to the use and storage of chemicals (see also **Hazardous substances**). Some chemicals such as medicines, cosmetics and pesticides are covered by separate specific laws.

References and further reading

Chemicals (Hazard Information and Packaging for Supply) Regulations 2009, SI 2009/716 (HMSO, London)

Control of Substances Hazardous to Health Regulations 2002, SI 2002/2677 (HMSO, London)

General duties, Health and Safety at Work etc Act 1974

Notification of New Substances Regulations 1993, SI 1993/3050 (HMSO, London)

Children

Children are one of the most vulnerable groups in society and child labour remains a global problem. In Britain children not of school leaving age may not work except in certain narrowly prescribed circumstances. However, injuries to children continue to occur from playing or trespassing on premises. Between 1993 and 2003, 35 children were killed and at least 400 injured on farms. In the last five years 530 children have been killed or injured on construction sites. Others are killed on railways.

Risk assessments should take this possibility into account. Steps should be taken to save children from their curiosity by ensuring that pits are fenced off, tanks securely covered and so on. It is the responsibility of operators and contractors to do their best to keep children off their sites and to store materials and plant safely away from them. A child was drowned in a cesspit that had been left uncovered on a caravan site. Even dumped, disused refrigerators have proved fatal to children.

See also **Young persons**.

References and further reading

General duties, Health and Safety at Work etc Act 1974

Management of Health and Safety Regulations 1999, SI 1999/3242 (HMSO, London)

HSE. *Protecting the public – your next move*, HSG151 (HSE Books, Sudbury, 1997)

Cold

See **Environmental conditions.**

Compressed air

Compressed air is used not only for powering hand tools and air lines and in special industrial handling applications, but also for keeping water out of tunnels or chambers under construction. As well as the obvious safety problems arising from pressure systems, working in compressed air can also present health problems:

- barotrauma, damage to air-containing cavities in the body
- decompression sickness ('the bends')
- dysbaric osteonecrosis, a condition which damages the bones and joints.

Misuse of airlines, for example in horseplay against fellow workers, can be very dangerous and cause serious injury.

The Construction (Health, Safety and Welfare) Regulations and Construction (Design and Management) Regulations apply to compressed air construction projects and the Work in Compressed Air Regulations apply additional requirements on compressed air contractors, including:

- safe systems of work
- medical surveillance and treatment
- HSE approval of compression and decompression procedures
- emergency procedures
- fire precautions
- provision of information, instruction and training
- health and exposure records.

See also **Diving**.

References and further reading

Construction (Design and Management) Regulations 2007, SI 2007/320 (HMSO, London)

HSE. *A guide to the Work in Compressed Air Regulations 1996 – guidance on Regulations*, L96 (HSE Books, Sudbury, 1996)

Work in Compressed Air Regulations 1996, SI 1996/1656 (HMSO, London)

Confined spaces

Many workers have lost their lives in confined spaces such as tanks, silos, sumps and closed vessels in a wide range of industries. On average, 15 people are killed every year from this cause. Entry is often necessary for cleaning and maintenance purposes but the presence of any residual toxic gases and vapours, or lack of oxygen, must be anticipated in planning the task. This may involve the need for testing and analysis. The Confined Spaces Regulations require employers to provide a safe system of work. As always, a risk assessment should be carried out and any necessary special precautions specified, such as the use of breathing and rescue apparatus and appropriate training for workers specific to their task. A 'permit to work' system will usually be necessary for this kind of work (see **Permits to work**). Training of workers and supervision by a competent manager are essential.

In the absence of appropriate training, an all too common accident may occur, when one worker attempts to rescue another in difficulty and is himself also overcome. Three men died in a single incident in 2004 when one man fell into a mobile slurry storage tank and his two colleagues tried to rescue him. They were overcome by fumes.

References and further reading

Confined Spaces Regulations 1997, SI 1997/1713 (HMSO, London)

HSE, free leaflet. *Safe work in confined spaces*, INDG258 (HSE Books, Sudbury, 1999)

HSE. *Safe work in confined spaces. Confined Spaces Regulations 1997 – Approved Code of Practice, Regulations and guidance*, L101 (HSE Books, Sudbury, 2009)

Construction

The construction sector includes many diverse activities, such as preparation of sites, building work, structural alterations, maintenance and cleaning of buildings and demolition work. The hazards encompass a very wide range, including falls from height, being struck by falling objects, trips and slips, manual handling, transport, machinery, electricity, fire, collapsing excavations and asbestos exposure.

In recent years, on average one or two workers have been killed on sites in Great Britain every week, constituting about a third of all workplace fatalities. In 2003/04, 70 out of the 235 fatalities to workers occurred in the construction industry.

The industry continues to have a very poor reputation for health and safety in spite of the high standards achieved by a few firms and the many initiatives pursued over the years. Notable among the latter was the introduction of the Construction (Design and Management) Regulations 1994, often referred to as the 'CDM Regulations', which attempted to improve the management of risks through involving designers, such as architects, and the clients. Designers and clients were given duties as well as employers, main or subcontractors and their workers.

In response to criticism of the regulations, the 1994 Regulations and the Construction (Health, Safety and Welfare) Regulations 1996 were replaced in 2007 by new CDM Regulations, supported by an Approved Code of Practice and revised guidance. These are intended to simplify requirements, focus attention on planning and management rather than the associated paperwork, and encourage better co-ordination and co-operation between designers and contractors. In 2001, the Strategic Forum for Construction committed the industry to a major change in performance through setting challenging targets and plans for action. These aimed to reduce:

- the incidence rate of fatalities and major injuries by 40 per cent by 2004/05 and 66 per cent by 2009/10
- the incidence rate of cases of work-related ill health by 20 per cent by 2004/05 and 50 per cent by 2009/10
- the number of working days lost from work-related injury and ill health by 20 per cent by 2004/05 and 50 per cent by 2009/10.

Even if a company carries out no construction work itself, it is vital to remember that if it lets out a contract for work on its premises it cannot assume that it can safely leave everything to the contractor. On the contrary, in the event of an accident, even if the company thought it was principally its contractor's fault, it would face difficult questions from investigators if unable to show that it had taken its legal duties seriously. See also **Contractors**.

Several sets of health and safety regulations apply to the construction industry. There is also a wealth of guidance available from the HSE, which works closely with the industry through the Construction Industry Advisory Committee (CONIAC) to prepare and disseminate good practice.

References and further reading

Confined Spaces Regulations 1997, SI 1997/1713 (HMSO, London)

Construction (Design and Management) Regulations 2007, SI 2007/320 (HMSO, London)

ConstructionSkills. Industry guidance on the Construction (Design and Management) Regulations 2007, www.cskills.org/healthsafety/cdmregulations.

HSE. *Fire safety in construction work. Guidance for clients, designers and those managing and carrying out construction work involving significant fire risks*, HSG168 (HSE Books, Sudbury, 1997)

HSE. *Health and safety in construction*, HSG150 (HSE Books, Sudbury, 2001)

HSE. *Health and safety in excavations: be safe and shore*, HSG185 (HSE Books, Sudbury, 1999)

HSE. *Health and safety in roof work*, HSG33 (HSE Books, Sudbury, 1998)

HSE. *Managing health and safety in construction. Construction (Design and Management) Regulations – Approved Code of Practice*, L144 (HSE Books, Sudbury, 2007)

HSE. *Workplace health, safety and welfare. Workplace (Health, Safety and Welfare) Regulations 1992 – Approved Code of Practice and guidance*, L24 (HSE Books, Sudbury, 1992)

Lifting Operations and Lifting Equipment Regulations 1998, SI 1998/2307 (HMSO, London)

Provision and Use of Work Equipment Regulations 1998, SI 1998/2306 (HMSO, London)

Work at Height Regulations 2005, SI 2005/735 (HMSO, London)

Workplace (Health, Safety and Welfare) Regulations 1992, SI 1992/3004 (HMSO, London)

Contractors

Many companies will use contractors to provide them with goods and services but give little thought to the consequences of a contractor having or causing an accident on the premises, assuming that it will not be their responsibility and that their own personnel, property and reputation will not be harmed. However, any contractor's poor performance could adversely affect the business.

By law, while contractors have their own duties towards their employees and others under health and safety law, when they are working on your site you have duties towards them and may well be liable if anything goes wrong. Establishing the right relationship between you and your contractors is the key to avoiding safety problems.

It is therefore worth confirming that your company has a formal process for checking the competence and track record of contractors in managing health and safety, that any hazards they may encounter on site have been properly communicated to them, and that responsibilities have been clearly understood and agreed between you.

A system is also needed for checking that your company's purchases of materials, equipment and services meet the necessary health and safety and environmental standards.

References and further reading

Management of Health and Safety at Work Regulations 1999, SI 1999/3242 (HMSO, London)

Health and Safety at Work etc Act 1974

HSE. *Successful health and safety management*, HSG65 (HSE Books, Sudbury, 2003)

HSE. *Managing contractors: a guide for employers*, HSG159 (HSE Books, Sudbury, 2000)

Institution of Occupational Safety and Health and American Society of Safety Engineers, free document. *Global best practices in contractor safety* (IOSH/ASSE, Leicester, 2003)

COSHH

See **Hazardous substances**.

Data protection

Considerable amounts of information relating to individuals are kept by companies, and problems can sometimes arise in relation to health and safety issues about release of data. Since March 2000, when the Data Protection Act 1998 (implementing a European Directive) came into force, employers and others who store personal data have been required to comply with certain principles requiring information to be:

- fairly and lawfully processed
- adequate, relevant and not excessive
- accurate
- not kept longer than necessary
- processed in accordance with employees' rights
- not transferred to countries without adequate protection.

Photographs and film records are also covered. A draft code of practice produced by the Information Commissioner suggests that routine CCTV monitoring is justified where risks to safety or security are likely.

References and further reading

Data Protection Act 1998

Information Commissioner's website, www.informationcommissioner.gov.uk

Dermatitis

Dermatitis, or skin disease, is a problem in almost every sector. Thirty-nine thousand people were estimated by the HSE in 2002 to be suffering from skin disease in Great Britain, with 3,900 new cases diagnosed every year.

Dermatitis is caused by contact with many types of dusts, fumes and liquids. These substances, depending on their potency, may cause damage immediately or after many weeks of exposure. Exposure to sunlight can also cause damage. Dermatitis usually affects the hands or forearms but may also affect the face, neck or chest, and even parts of the body that have not been exposed to the irritating substance. Symptoms include itching, scaling, blistering and reddening of skin. In bad cases the skin will crack and bleed. Some people are affected for life. It can be very painful, but dermatitis is not infectious.

It can affect people working in almost every business sector, but the higher risk sectors are:

- hair dressing and beauty care
- catering and food processing
- cleaning
- construction
- engineering
- printing
- chemicals

- healthcare
- agriculture/horticulture
- rubber
- offshore.

However, dermatitis is highly preventable. Prevention of harmful exposure is usually reasonably practicable, eg by use of protective clothing, barrier creams and washing thoroughly after contact with harmful substances.

Under the general duties of the 1974 Act and the Management of Health and Safety at Work Regulations, employers have a legal obligation to protect the health and safety of their workers. The COSHH Regulations also apply to chemicals and implement the health requirements of the EC Chemical Agents Directive.

References and further reading

General duties, Health and Safety at Work etc Act 1974

Management of Health and Safety Regulations 1999, SI 1999/3242 (HMSO, London)

Control of Substances Hazardous to Health Regulations 2002, SI 2002/2677 (HMSO, London)

Personal Protective Equipment at Work Regulations 1992, SI 1992/2966 (HMSO, London)

European Commission. Chemical Agents Directive 98/24/EC (*Official Journal of the European Communities*, 7 April 1998)

Disability

The employment provisions of the Disability Discrimination Act (DDA) came into effect in December 1996 and with its associated regulations introduced measures to end discrimination against disabled persons. The Act came fully into effect in October 2004, when it required all workplaces and service providers' premises to be fully accessible to the disabled.

The law is enforced through the Employment Tribunal system and defines disability as a physical or mental impairment which has substantial and long term adverse effects on a person's ability to carry out normal day-to-day activities.

As well as access and egress, other physical features of sites and buildings arising from their design, construction and the layout of furniture and equipment may need to be assessed and adjusted where this is reasonable.

References and further reading

Disability Discrimination Act 1995

Disability Discrimination (Employment) Regulations 1996, SI 1996/1456 (HMSO, London)

Disability Discrimination (Meaning of Disability) Regulations 1996, SI 1996/1455 (HMSO, London)

Display screen equipment

Display screen equipment, colloquially known as VDUs (visual display units) are the subject of a European Directive intended to control risks from this kind of equipment. The Health and Safety (Display Screen Equipment) Regulations implemented the Directive in Britain and require employers to:

- carry out an analysis of workstations and assess risks
- see that workstations comply with the provisions relating to screen, keyboard, work surface, chair, space, lighting, reflections, glare, noise, heat, radiation, humidity, systems and software
- reduce risks as low as reasonably practicable
- arrange eye and eyesight tests
- provide any special corrective appliance
- provide employees with training on health and safety aspects of workstations
- provide health and safety information to operators and users.

Eyestrain, musculoskeletal disorders (MSDs), repetitive strain injuries (RSIs) and work-related upper limb disorders (WRULDs) are commonly associated with this kind of work. In a recent campaign the HSE visited 8,000 workplaces and issued 200 improvement and prohibition notices requiring employers to take remedial actions.

A company that follows the guidance and codes of practice issued to assist compliance with these regulations will normally be doing what is required to reduce risks as low as reasonably practicable.

Reference and further reading

Health and Safety (Display Screen Equipment) Regulations 1992 (amended in 2002), SI 1992/2792 (HMSO, London)

HSE, free leaflet. *Aching arms (or RSI) in small businesses*, INDG171 (HSE Books, Sudbury, 2003)

HSE. *The law on VDUs: an easy guide*, HSG90 (HSE Books, Sudbury, 2003)

HSE, free leaflet. *Working with VDUs*, INDG36 (HSE Books, Sudbury, 1998)

Diving

Between 1997 and 2004, 24 divers died in accidents, several being members of the public under training by professional instructors for recreational diving. Others were commercial divers in inshore and deep diving activities.

As well as the general duties of the 1974 Act, the Diving at Work Regulations specifically cover this hazardous activity. There are also five sector-specific codes of practice which provide detailed guidance for the safe conduct of diving.

Diving is a specialised operation that must be entrusted to competent persons. The client for diving services must appoint a competent contractor who in turn appoints a diving supervisor. The client must also ensure that the site is safe to use, tell the contractor about any known hazards at the site, and support the supervisor and contractor in the event of an emergency.

The diving contractor plans and conducts the diving project. He has the main responsibility under the regulations to ensure that the project is safely conducted, including assessing risks, taking all the necessary special precautions to protect the safety of the divers and appointing a supervisor.

The supervisor, who must be qualified and competent, is in charge of the dive. The divers also have responsibilities, including holding an approved diving qualification and a valid medical certificate. Diver competence standards are administered by the HSE, which is responsible for the inspection of occupational diving. Recreational diving, increasingly popular, is subject to inspection by local authorities.

References and further reading

Diving at Work Regulations 1997, SI 1997/2776 (HMSO, London)

HSE. *Commercial diving projects offshore* (L103), *Commercial diving projects inland/inshore* (L104), *Recreational diving projects* (L105), *Media diving projects* (L106) and *Scientific and archaeological diving projects* (L107): all Approved Codes of Practice to the Diving at Work Regulations 1997 (all HSE Books, Sudbury, 1998)

HSE. *Managing health and safety at recreational dive sites*, HSG240 (HSE Books, Sudbury, 2003)

Driving

About 3,500 people are killed every year and 40,000 seriously injured on Britain's roads. There are 250,000 incidents and 300,000 casualties altogether. The direct costs of accidents that cause injury are estimated at about £3 billion a year.

Research has found that about a third of these incidents are work-related. Higher mileage drivers are as likely to be killed doing their job as workers in high-hazard industries such as quarrying. Company car drivers are thought to be 50 per cent more likely to be involved in an accident than owner-drivers.

In its strategy 'Tomorrow's roads: safer for everyone', published in 2000, the government set a target of a 40 per cent reduction in deaths and serious injuries from road accidents by 2010. A government-appointed task group has concluded that existing law adequately covers the risks to workers but needs to be more consistently and universally applied.

Companies that have large goods vehicles or passenger service vehicles will need to comply with legal requirements specific to those. Drivers are responsible for the way they drive and for complying with road traffic laws and the Highway Code, but employers have duties towards their employees under health and safety law. It is not enough simply to see that vehicles such as vans or company cars have an MOT certificate and their drivers a valid licence. The Management Regulations apply and employers should assess the risks to which they are exposing their drivers and ensure that they are trained and their vehicles are well maintained. They should also be careful not to impose unrealistic delivery schedules.

See also **Mobile phones.**

References and further reading

General duties, Health and Safety at Work etc Act 1974

HSE, free leaflet. *Driving at work: managing work-related road safety,* INDG382 (HSE Books, Sudbury, 2003)

Management of Health and Safety at Work Regulations 1999, SI 1999/3242 (HMSO, London)

Road Traffic Acts 1988 and 1991 (HMSO, London)

Royal Society for the Prevention of Accidents. *Managing occupational road risk* (RoSPA, 2003)

The Stationery Office. *The Highway Code* (TSO, London, 2007)

Drugs

Abuse of drugs and other substances is likely to occur in today's workplaces and can be a root cause of accidents, bullying, violence and stress. Managers need to be on the lookout for signs of these problems, encourage workers to seek expert help and be supportive while they do.

Managers should also be prepared to take disciplinary action where safety is in jeopardy, for the sake both of the company's reputation and the health and safety of other personnel. This is more likely to succeed after first gaining the consent of the workforce to a drugs policy. The HSE has published free advice, 'Drugs misuse at work: a guide for employers', which explains how to introduce a policy based on four steps:

- find out if there is a problem
- if so, decide what to do about it
- take action
- check what you have done.

Drugs, like alcohol, are known to affect judgment and co-ordination and increase risks of an accident, particularly in safety-critical work. Short of that, drugs can reduce work performance, and a drinking culture can give customers a bad impression of the company.

Employers have a general duty under the 1974 Act to ensure so far as is reasonably practicable the health, safety and welfare of employees. The risk assessment requirements of the Management Regulations apply. If an employer knows that employees are under the influence of drugs or alcohol, allowing them to continue working could expose them and others to risk and would be in breach of the law.

Employees themselves have a general duty not to endanger themselves and others. It is also a criminal offence under the Transport and Works Act 1992 for certain workers to be unfit through drink or drugs while working on railways and similar safety-critical transport systems, and operators must show all due diligence in preventing an offence from being committed.

Drugs screening can be carried out, but this is a sensitive issue which in order to succeed should first receive the consent of the workforce to the policy.

See also **Alcohol**.

References and further reading

General duties, Health and Safety at Work etc Act 1974

HSE, free leaflet. *Drugs misuse at work: a guide for employers*, INDG91 (HSE Books, Sudbury, 1998)

Management of Health and Safety at Work Regulations 1999, SI 1999/3242 (HMSO, London)

Electricity

Electricity is pretty much taken for granted but it kills about 30 people every year at work through shocks and burns, and about 1,000 people are injured. Contact with live parts, explosions caused by electrical equipment, ignition of flammable liquids or vapours by static electricity, and fires caused by faulty equipment are the principal hazards.

Half of the deaths are caused by contact with or flashover from close proximity to overhead lines. Striking underground cables during digging operations is another risk to be avoided by use of detection methods.

The normal voltage of 240 volts is capable of killing people with only 14 milliamps of current. Portable equipment is often involved in accidents and the risk is increased when it is used in confined spaces among earthed metalwork, or out of doors in damp conditions. Residual current circuit breakers and double insulated tools can help but low-voltage portable tools (110 volts through an isolating transformer) or rechargeable battery operated tools are preferable in these circumstances, particularly where hard usage is expected, as on building sites. Exterior site lighting is generally safe and effective if at low voltage (12 or 25 volts).

Where electrical equipment has to be used in wet conditions or in a flammable or explosive atmosphere such as in mines with a methane gas hazard, offshore oil and gas installations, flammable paint spraying or flammable dust processing, specially protected equipment is necessary. Installing and maintaining this is a job obviously requiring specialist attention.

The Electricity at Work Regulations set out the legal requirements for protection against these hazards. Insulation, protection and earthing of live equipment is generally necessary. No one should work on or near live equipment unless it is really essential and special precautions are taken.

Good maintenance of electrical equipment is necessary to prevent danger. Equipment should be regularly inspected and tested to identify and remedy any physical damage to supply cables and identify earthing problems which can arise from corrosion, vibration or mechanical failure.

Control measures for portable tools include:

- use of low voltage equipment
- use of residual current circuit-breaking devices which trip when there is a fault
- use of double-insulated tools.

To avoid the risk of flashover, work should not be conducted within 9 metres of overhead lines unless special precautions have been taken. Work in the vicinity of underground cables requires special care to avoid cable strikes.

It is vital that people carrying out electrical work are competent to do so safely. Electrical work is often contracted out and it is essential to employ competent contractors. The National Inspection Council for Electrical Installation Contracting (NICEIC) is a source of information about competent persons and checks their work from time to time.

References and further reading

Electricity at Work Regulations 1989, SI 1989/635 (HMSO, London)

Electrical Equipment (Safety) Regulations 1994, SI 1994/3260 (HMSO, London)

Equipment and Protective Systems Intended for Use in Potentially Explosive Atmospheres Regulations 1996, SI 1996/192 (HMSO, London)

HSE. *Memorandum of guidance on the Electricity at Work Regulations 1989*, HSR25 (HSE Books, Sudbury, 1989)

Environmental conditions

Extremes of heat and cold and humidity can affect human performance and cause health and safety problems. Heat can be extremely fatiguing, particularly if accompanied by high humidity. Cold can cause mistakes to be made in handling and operating dangerous machinery such as circular saws and hand tools. High relative humidity may need to be controlled, particularly if humid conditions are required for process purposes. Expert opinion suggests that in the UK the acceptable 'thermal comfort zone' for most people is between 13 and 30 degrees Celsius.

The general duties of the 1974 Act, the risk assessment requirements of the Management Regulations and the Workplace (Health and Safety) Regulations apply. The Workplace Regulations require the temperature to be reasonable during working hours in all workplaces inside buildings.

The accompanying approved code of practice makes it clear that what 'reasonable' means may depend on the kind of workplace, eg a cold store, foundry, kitchen or office. The temperature in workrooms should provide 'reasonable comfort' without the need for special clothing but where this is impractical because of hot or cold processes all reasonable steps should be taken to achieve a temperature which is as close as possible to 'comfortable'.

A workroom means a room where people normally work for more than just short periods. There are no maximum limits set for temperature but workrooms should be at least 16 degrees Celsius unless much of the work involves severe physical effort, in which case it should be at least 13 degrees Celsius.

Bear in mind that other factors like excessive humidity or inadequate air movement can exacerbate the effects of high temperature on human performance. Steps can be taken to achieve a comfortable environment by insulating hot equipment, installing air cooling plant, improving general ventilation and providing local cooling by fans. If necessary, other measures such as provision of suitable protective clothing, rest facilities and rotation of tasks may be required to reduce the length of exposure to uncomfortable conditions.

Lighting also needs consideration. There are no statutory levels set but adequate levels of lighting will differ according to the kind of premises and tasks in question. Fine work will obviously require a higher level of lighting than general working areas, but too much light can be as problematic as too little. Glare should be avoided. Stairs, corridors and any other areas where there could be a risk of slips and trips should be kept well lit.

See also **Sick building syndrome**.

References and further reading

General duties, Health and Safety at Work etc Act 1974

HSE, free leaflet. *Heat stress in the workplace – what you need to know as an employer*, GEIS1 (HSE website, www.hse.gov.uk)

HSE. *Lighting at work*, HSG38 (HSE Books, Sudbury, 1998)

HSE. *Thermal comfort in the workplace – guidance for employers*, HSG194 (HSE Books, Sudbury, 1999)

HSE. *Workplace health, safety and welfare. Workplace (Health, Safety and Welfare) Regulations 1992 – Approved Code of Practice and guidance*, L24 (HSE Books, Sudbury, 1992)

Management of Health and Safety at Work Regulations 1999, SI 1999/3242 (HMSO, London)

Workplace (Health, Safety and Welfare) Regulations 1992, SI 1992/3004 (HMSO, London)

Ergonomics

Back pain, musculoskeletal disorders, repetitive strain injury, work-related upper limb disorders, carpal tunnel syndrome, and strains and sprains acquired at work cause millions of days of lost working time each year. They usually have their origin in poorly designed systems of work, work stations or practices such as incorrect lifting techniques.

More than a third of over three-day injuries are thought to be the result of poor practices in manual handling operations.

Ergonomics, sometimes known as 'human factors', is a fairly recent science, defined by some as the scientific study of human work. Ergonomists examine the anatomical, biomechanical, physiological, psychological and social features of the individual's constitution within the system of work and take the view that the job should be designed to fit the person, rather than the other way around, which uses techniques such as selection and training to fit the person to the job.

See also **Human factors, Repetitive strain injury** and **Work-related upper limb disorders.**

References and further reading

HSE. *A pain in your workplace? Ergonomic problems and solutions*, HSG121 (HSE Books, Sudbury, 1994)

HSE, free leaflet. *Getting to grips with manual handling – a short guide for employers*, INDG143 (HSE Books, Sudbury, 2004)

HSE. *Upper limb disorders in the workplace – a guide to prevention*, HSG60 (HSE Books, Sudbury, 2002)

Management of Health and Safety at Work Regulations 1999, SI 1999/3242 (HMSO, London)

Manual Handling Operations Regulations 1992, SI 1992/2793 (HMSO, London)

McKeown, C and Twiss, M. *Workplace ergonomics: a practical guide* (IOSH Services, Leicester, 2004)

Stubbs, Prof. D. *Why we need ergonomics* (Robens Institute of Industrial and Environmental Health and Safety, University of Surrey, 1994)

Experts

Experts have a valuable role in helping to manage risks but expert opinion can often differ when risk is being quantified or control measures selected, and crucially about whether the 'ALARP' principle (reducing risks as low as reasonably practicable) has been achieved, and thus compliance with the law. When, for example, an inspector is considering whether a company is complying fully with legal requirements he or she will have to decide whether the risks are being controlled ALARP, which will require at least these to be evident:

- a suitable and sufficient assessment of the risks
- evidence of good practice in controlling risks
- evidence of specific measures to control specific risks.

Experts will also be considering how big or significant the risks actually are and what is generally accepted to be good practice in controlling them. Deciding whether all this adds up to being ALARP often requires a combination of technical and legal expertise with practical understanding of the situation in which the risks arise.

Deciding what is ALARP can thus become a complex and difficult question, particularly where there may be uncertainty about the data, eg scientific or medical evidence, and the precautionary principle of erring on the side of safety needs to be followed. Conflict can arise in making decisions and if things later go wrong directors, managers and experts may all have to share the blame. A classic example is the Challenger Space Shuttle disaster in 1986, when against advice a launch took place in poor weather conditions after a series of problems had caused delay. A component failure caused the rocket to explode, killing all seven astronauts. The root cause was said to be an organisational culture driving the decision to launch.

It is helpful for organisations that are likely to have to deal internally with the more complex questions about risk to have conflict resolution procedures in place.

Companies may sometimes disagree with a decision taken by the regulator. Regulatory decisions, eg whether or not to accept a safety case, can always be tested as a last resort in the courts, possibly by judicial review of the decision or by making an appeal against an enforcement notice. Appeals against inspectors' notices do not often succeed and it is invariably better if matters can be resolved informally through discussion at an earlier stage.

References and further reading

HSE Research report. *Dealing with differences of expert opinion*, RR012 (HSE website, www.hse.gov.uk/research/rrhtm/rr012.htm, 2002)

Explosives

The Explosives Act 1875 was one of the first pieces of safety legislation to deal with the control of major hazards. Amended in 1923, it became one of the 'relevant statutory provisions' under the 1974 Act. Since then the hazard from explosives, which are commonly used in mining, quarrying, tunnelling, civil engineering and demolition, has attracted a suite of regulations covering classification, packaging, labelling, transportation and control.

The manufacture, storage and use of explosives are strictly controlled by licensing and accidents are rare if the proper precautions are taken. However, mistakes can be devastating. An explosion at ICI's Cook's Works during the mixing of nitro-glycerine destroyed the plant entirely. In 1989, a van carrying poorly packed explosives caught fire and exploded, killing a fireman, after entering a factory yard in Peterborough. The jolt from passing over a speed ramp was sufficient to ignite the load.

New regulations controlling the manufacture and storage of explosives, amending the Explosives Act 1875 and associated legislation, were laid before Parliament in April 2005. An approved code of practice is also to be produced.

See also **Fireworks.**

References and further reading

Explosives Acts 1875 and 1923

Classification and Labelling of Explosives Regulations 1983, SI 1983/1140 (HMSO, London)

Control of Explosives Regulations 1991, SI 1991/1531 (HMSO, London)

Packaging of Explosives for Carriage Regulations 1991, SI 1991/2097 (HMSO, London)

Chemicals (Hazard Information and Packaging for Supply) Regulations 2009, SI 2009/716 (HMSO, London)

Dangerous Substances and Explosive Atmospheres Regulations 2002, SI 2002/2776 (HMSO, London)

Manufacture and Storage of Explosives Regulations 2005, SI 2005/1082 (HMSO, London)

Falls from height

The force of gravity was a factor in the deaths of 58 workers in 2007/08. Causes are more often poor management control than equipment failure. Common root causes found by investigations include failures to anticipate that there could be a problem, to ensure that safe systems of work are provided and followed, to provide information, instruction, training and supervision, and to provide safe equipment and see that it is used.

About half of the fatal falls occur in the construction industry. The main cause of injury from falls across all sectors is falling from ladders (about 1,000 of all fatal and major injuries occur in this way each year).

Building work, roof maintenance and repair, demolition activities and dock work are obvious areas for close attention, but activities such as cleaning, electrical maintenance and sheeting of high vehicles also present potential risks that need assessment and consideration during the review of control measures.

Falling through fragile roofs is an all too common cause of fatalities. Fragile roofs such as those made of asbestos cement, glass and other materials that cannot bear a person's weight must be identified. Safe access and a safe place of work should be provided if it is necessary to approach or cross fragile materials, and edge protection should be provided where necessary.

Contractors visiting a company's sites may also be at risk. Companies need to have systems which take account of this during procurement, and they must control and monitor their contractors if they have to work at height.

The law on working at height has recently been changed in Great Britain in response to a European Directive. The new regulations came into force in April 2005 and drew together all existing law on the subject.

Under the new Work at Height Regulations the old '2-metre' rule of thumb suggesting a division between 'low' and 'high' falls has been removed, as more injuries occur from low falls than from falls from above 2 metres. HSE guidance on the new regulations advises that risk assessments need to be carried out for any work at height, which should be planned, organised and carried out by competent organisations. The right work equipment and measures such as provision of guardrails and working platforms should be employed before other measures such as nets or airbags, which may only mitigate the distance and consequences of a fall.

See also **Fragile roofs, Ladders.**

References and further reading

European Commission. Temporary Working at Height Directive 2001/45/EC (*Official Journal of the European Communities*, 27 June 2001)

Health and Safety at Work etc Act 1974

HSE. *The Work at Height Regulations 2005 – a brief guide*, INDG401 (HSE Books, Sudbury, 2005)

HSE, free leaflet. *Working on roofs*, INDG284 (HSE Books, Sudbury, 1999)

Lifting Operations and Lifting Equipment Regulations 1998, SI 1998/2307 (HMSO, London)

Provision and Use of Work Equipment Regulations 1998, SI 1998/2306 (HMSO, London)

Work at Height Regulations 2005, SI 2005/735 (HMSO, London)

Fire and explosion

There have been many fires causing major loss of life and property damage in recent years. The circumstances can be unpredictable and usually take people by surprise.

A fire at Bradford City FC's football stadium in 1985 killed 56 people and injured 265. Flames and dense smoke overcame the victims very rapidly after rubbish which had accumulated under the wooden stand over many years caught fire. A public inquiry was held and a subsequent civil action challenged the responsibility of several parties including the fire safety enforcing authorities. Substantial compensation was paid to the families of victims.

A fire which started in the motor room of a wooden escalator at King's Cross underground station in 1987 caught rush hour travellers by surprise when flames roared up the escalator shaft from below and burst into the booking hall. Thirty-one people were killed. A public inquiry into the disaster recommended major changes in the regulation of fire safety, and smoking was banned on the Underground.

In 1984, a warehouse in Brightside Lane, Sheffield, containing a large quantity of miscellaneous chemicals and other goods burnt fiercely for days, resisting attempts to bring the fire under control, and releasing a cocktail of fumes and asbestos material from the building's structure over a wide area downwind. An investigation report by the HSE recommended improvements to firefighting practice and warehouse safety.

A vessel which contained flammable sludge ignited during a cleaning operation at a chemical works in Castleford in 1992. A fierce jet of flame erupted from the vessel like a blow-torch, destroying a control room in its path and striking an office building some distance away. Five workers died and the company concerned was prosecuted for a breach of health and safety law after an HSE investigation.

One of the worst events in recent memory was the explosion followed by raging fires which completely destroyed the Piper Alpha North Sea oil installation in 1988, killing 167 workers. A public inquiry led by Lord Cullen recommended major changes in the regulation of offshore safety, which was transferred from the oil industry's sponsor department, the Department of Energy, to the HSE.

Invariably with hindsight it is possible to see how these events might have been prevented. Fire is a menace in any workplace, whether or not highly flammable substances are being used or stored. The presence of substances such as paints and thinners, polystyrene packaging materials or polyurethane foam will obviously increase the risk. But even apparently low-risk workplaces will have sufficient combustible materials present, either in the production process or in the fabric of the building, to allow them to burn well and generate enough suffocating smoke and toxic fumes to threaten the lives of the people working inside. Risk assessment enables preventive action to be planned and implemented. This can save lives and avoid incurring the high costs of property damage and business interruption.

Suitable and sufficient fire precautions are therefore essential both to prevent fires from occurring and, if the worst still happens, to ensure that there is no loss of life. This requires installation and regular testing of an effective warning system, provision of suitable firefighting equipment, maintenance of adequate means of escape free from obstruction, and proper training in evacuation procedures for staff.

Before October 2006, most premises of any size required a fire certificate under the Fire Precautions Act, usually issued by the fire authority after an inspection. Even if a fire certificate was not required, a fire risk assessment had to be carried out under the Fire Precautions (Workplace) Regulations (as amended). However, the Regulatory Reform (Fire Safety) Order has made fire safety law easier to understand and comply with by bringing together fire safety legislation previously contained in over 100 separate pieces of legislation. Fire certificates have been abolished and a 'responsible person' for each premises is now required to carry out an assessment of the risk and take steps to remove or reduce it.

Storage of flammable materials inside workshops should be kept to the minimum necessary for reasonable use. Sources of ignition should be eliminated if possible or, if necessary for production processes, should be well protected. Remember that a source of ignition will almost always be found if there is a release of flammable liquid or vapour, so accidental release should be prevented through the safe design of plant. For example, non-spill containers are available for flammable liquids used on benches, and storage tanks can be bunded, ie protected by a continuous wall designed to contain the contents in the event of leakage.

The risk of explosion can exist in many circumstances. Explosions can be caused by ignition of flammable liquids, vapours, gases and dusts such as flour or custard powder, including finely ground metals such as aluminium and magnesium. Where premises are not kept clean and dust builds up on shelves and ledges overhead, a small explosion in an individual piece of machinery can shake down a cloud of flammable dust and cause a much larger secondary explosion, which may well destroy the building. These events are similar to the coal dust explosions which have caused major loss of life in underground mines.

There are well-tried and proven methods for suppressing explosions and for providing explosion relief on plant and in buildings. This is, of course, a job for specialist contractors.

The Electricity at Work Regulations (see **Electricity**) require special protection of electrical equipment used in flammable or explosive atmospheres.

There are many sources of advice about fire and explosion risks and precautions, and a number of specific legal provisions. Companies should bear in mind that the local fire authorities are normally the enforcing authority for fire safety, rather than the HSE. In addition, in certain circumstances, for example if your company is operating a major hazard site, the HSE will have responsibilities for enforcing controls over process fire risks.

References and further reading

Dangerous Substances and Explosive Atmospheres Regulations 2002, SI 2002/2776 (HMSO, London)

Electricity at Work Regulations 1989, SI 1989/635 (HMSO, London)

HSE. *Fire and explosion. How safe is your workplace?*, INDG370 (HSE Books, Sudbury, 2002)

Regulatory Reform (Fire Safety) Order 2005, SI 2005/1541 (HMSO, London)

The Stationery Office. *Fire safety: an employer's guide* (TSO, London, 1999)

Fireworks

The Explosives Act 1875 stipulates that manufacture and dismantling of fireworks may only be carried out in premises licensed under that Act. Fireworks may also be stored only on licensed or registered premises, though under the Control of Explosives Act 1991 this does not apply to fireworks intended for private use.

Companies may become involved in organising firework displays. These are covered by the 1974 Act if they involve a work activity. The Act will apply even if only one worker is involved in the display. Organisers have a duty to protect everyone present.

See also **Explosives**.

References and further reading

Control of Explosives Regulations 1991, SI 1991/1531 (HMSO, London)

Explosives Act 1875, as amended by the Explosives Act 1923

Fireworks Act 2003

Firework Safety Regulations 1997, SI 1997/2294 (HMSO, London)

General duties, Health and Safety at Work etc Act 1974

First aid

The Health and Safety (First Aid) Regulations require employers to provide adequate and appropriate equipment, facilities and personnel to enable first aid to be given to employees if they are injured or become ill at work.

Employers should carry out an assessment of first aid needs, which will depend on the circumstances found in different workplaces. This assessment will decide what is to be kept in first aid boxes, and whether a first aid room and trained first aiders are needed.

There are specific requirements for diving and for the offshore oil and gas industry.

References and further reading

Health and Safety (First Aid) Regulations 1981, SI 1981/917 (HMSO, London)

Reporting of Injuries, Diseases and Dangerous Occurrences Regulations 1995, SI 1995/3163 (HMSO, London)

HSE. *First aid at work. The Health and Safety (First Aid) Regulations 1981 – Approved Code of Practice and guidance*, L74 (HSE Books, Sudbury, 1997)

HSE. *First aid at work – your questions answered*, INDG214 (HSE Books, Sudbury, 1997)

Forklift trucks

Commonly used throughout industry, forklift trucks cause numerous injuries every year from poor maintenance and bad driving.

Forklift trucks should be regarded as lifting machinery, be kept well maintained and be thoroughly examined by someone competent to do so from time to time.

They should be driven only by competent drivers. Drivers should be properly trained by a training provider accredited by the HSE and should then be authorised by their employer before they are allowed to drive forklift trucks. Competence should be kept up by refresher training.

See also **Vehicles**.

References and further reading

Provision and Use of Work Equipment Regulations 1998, SI 1998/2306 (HMSO, London)

Lifting Operations and Lifting Equipment Regulations 1998, SI 1998/2307 (HMSO, London)

HSE. *Rider-operated lift trucks: operator training. Approved Code of Practice and guidance*, L117 (HSE Books, Sudbury, 1999)

Fragile roofs

The roofs of many industrial and commercial premises have been built from materials which, while designed to be weatherproof, cannot safely bear the weight of a person. Many workers have fallen to their deaths when roofing material has suddenly given way during maintenance or cleaning activities. Fragile roofs should be identified and plainly signed. Where it is necessary to approach them risks should first be properly assessed and appropriate safe access must be provided, such as a permanent walkway with guard rails, or temporary crawling boards.

Health and safety law requires safe access and a safe place of work and inspectors investigating a fatal accident following a breach of the law involving such an obviously preventable event are almost certain to prosecute. The courts are likely to impose a severe penalty.

See also **Falls from height, Construction**

References and further reading

Management of Health and Safety at Work Regulations 1999, SI 1999/3242 (HMSO, London)

Work at Height Regulations 2005, SI 2005/735 (HMSO, London)

HSE, free leaflet. *Working on roofs*, INDG 284 (HSE Books, Sudbury, 1999)

Gas

Gas used as an industrial fuel tends to be either mains supplied natural gas (methane) or LPG (butane, propane) stored in bulk containers or cylinders. There are obvious fire and explosion hazards to be controlled.

LPG stored in very large quantities will attract the requirements of the Control of Major Accident Hazards Regulations ('COMAH' – see Chapter 14).

Mains gas enters premises through service pipes connected to high, medium or low pressure mains in the national gas transmission system, which still contains cast-iron mains laid down decades ago. Serious gas explosions have occurred when service pipes have been damaged or cast-iron mains have been fractured by ground movement occurring naturally or caused by heavy vehicular traffic, for example at Putney in 1985 when eight people were killed in a block of flats. Accidents have also occurred when ductile iron mains have corroded. There is an ongoing programme to replace old gas mains with durable polyethylene plastic piping.

Gas-fired equipment such as drying ovens will need flame failure devices, explosion relief and regular maintenance and cleaning to ensure safety in use.

For toxic or flammable gases and fumes: see **Hazardous substances** and **Fires and explosions**.

References and further reading:
General duties, Health and Safety at Work etc Act 1974
Management of Health and Safety at Work Regulations 1999, SI 1999/3242 (HMSO, London)
Gas Safety (Management) Regulations 1996, SI 1996/551 (HMSO, London)
Pipelines Safety Regulations 1996, SI 1996/825 (HMSO, London)
Control of Major Accident Hazards Regulations 1999, SI 1999/743 (HMSO, London)
Control of Major Accident Hazards (Amendment) Regulations 2005, SI 2005/1088 (HMSO, London)

Genetically modified organisms

Genetically modified organisms have been the subject of scare stories. However, most work with GMOs in contained use is inherently safe because it involves the insertion of genes into micro-organisms that have been deliberately disabled so that they cannot grow outside the test tube environment.

Risk assessments for work that does not fall into this category have to be sent to regulatory authorities for approval before work can commence. Approval takes into account the efficacy of proposed containment measures and errs on the side of safety where there is any uncertainty (the 'precautionary principle').

The Department for Environment, Food and Rural Affairs is responsible for the control of deliberate releases of GMOs. There is also legislation covering the environmental risks posed by work in contained facilities with genetically modified plants and animals.

References and further reading

Genetically Modified Organisms (Contained Use) Regulations 2000, SI 2000/2831 (HMSO, London)

Genetically Modified Organisms (Deliberate Release) Regulations 2002, SI 2002/2443 (HMSO, London)

Environmental Protection Act 1990, Section 108 (1)

Hazardous substances

Many thousands of people are exposed to chemicals and other hazardous substances in the course of their work. Failure to prevent or properly control exposure can result in:

- injury, serious illness or death
- lost earnings
- reduced productivity
- claims for compensation
- criminal prosecutions
- sickness benefit costs.

The effects of exposure can include:

- dermatitis
- asthma
- being overcome by fumes
- acid burns
- poisoning
- lung disease
- cancer.

The costs of ill health at work to British society in 2001/02 were estimated by the HSE at £11–17 billion. Exposure to hazardous substances is a substantial contributor. At individual company and plant levels, the share of these costs can be very significant.

The Control of Substances Hazardous to Health Regulations 2002 (COSHH) are a key part of the legal framework for the protection of health at work. There are proposals to amend these key regulations but, at the moment, complying with COSHH generally involves:

- assessing the risks to health
- deciding what precautions are needed
- preventing or controlling exposure
- ensuring that control measures are used and maintained properly
- monitoring exposure of workers to hazardous substances
- carrying out appropriate health surveillance where necessary
- ensuring that employees are properly informed, trained and supervised.

In a large organisation with complex processes, it is likely that some of this work will need to be done by competent people with appropriate expertise, either employed in-house or contracted in from a specialist consultancy. Nevertheless, during the risk assessment it is always worthwhile for the management to consult the company's employees and safety representatives who are working with the substances. They often know more about them than their managers. Many companies fail to involve their own workers in assessments, which is a mistake. In any event, by law employees must be informed of the results.

Risks to employees who visit other firms' sites must also be assessed – their employer as well as the site operator is responsible for ensuring they have the necessary protection. Companies should also bear in mind risks to members of the public and others, including contractors, who might be exposed to substances on or from their premises.

The nature of the hazard from different substances varies greatly. Some, such as toxic solvents, can have serious ill effects if they are inhaled, absorbed through the skin or ingested in small quantities over a long period. Others, such as strong acids, can cause immediate trauma, while others, such as some isocyanates, can sensitise someone for life in one small exposure. Some carcinogenic substances are regarded as so dangerous that they have been banned from industrial use.

With the right precautions, it is possible to work safely with the most dangerous substances and prevent harm from occurring. It is therefore vital that all the substances and their hazardous properties are properly identified before risk assessments are carried out, as failure to understand the hazard will result in inaccurate assessment of the risk and selection of the wrong control measures, leading to inadequate control.

Workplace exposure limits (WELs) have been set for many substances in the light of extensive research and testing. Information about WELs is published by the HSE.

The 'cocktail effect' is an expression sometimes used for situations where a number of chemicals become mixed and it is difficult to determine the exact consequences of exposure to the mixture.

The 'precautionary principle', or erring on the side of safety, is another expression often used in connection with the control of hazardous substances. It should be applied whenever there is doubt.

There are a few exceptions to the application of the COSHH Regulations. For example, asbestos and lead are subject to separate, specific regulations (see **Asbestos, Lead**).

References and further reading

Chemicals (Hazard Information and Packaging for Supply) Regulations 2009, SI 2009/716 (HMSO, London)

Control of Asbestos Regulations 2006, SI 2006/2739 (HMSO, London)

Control of Lead at Work Regulations 2002, SI 2002/2676 (HMSO, London)

Control of Substances Hazardous to Health Regulations 2002, SI 2002/2677 (HMSO, London)

Control of Substances Hazardous to Health (Amendment) Regulations 2004, SI 2004/3386 (HMSO, London)

HSE. COSHH Essentials website, www.coshh-essentials.org.uk

HSE. *A step-by-step guide to COSHH assessment*, HSG97 (HSE Books, Sudbury, 2004)

HSE. *Interim update of the 'Costs to Britain of workplace accidents and work-related ill health'* (HSE Books, 2004)

HSE. *Workplace exposure limits*, EH40 (HSE Books, Sudbury, 2005)

Heat

See **Environmental conditions.**

Home workers

Data from the Census and Labour Force Survey indicate that the numbers of people working at home are increasing and doubled between 1981 and 1998 to about 2.5 per cent of the workforce. More and more companies are employing part-time workers, many of whom work at home.

Employers have responsibilities for self-employed workers. Even if a person working under the control and direction of a company is treated as self-employed for tax and national insurance purposes, they should be treated as an employee for health and safety purposes.

While the employer's duty of care applies wherever employees are working, some regulations, such as the Workplace (Health, Safety and Welfare) Regulations 1992, which set out minimum standards, do not apply to home working.

However, the Management of Health and Safety at Work Regulations 1999 do apply to home workers and require a risk assessment to be carried out. This needs to cover matters such as heating, lighting, ventilation, fire safety, electricity, equipment such as computers and workstations and any hazardous substances used or stored.

Sectors such as textiles, packaging, assembling or finishing, electrical or electronic assembly, business services and computers have been growth areas for home working. While hazards in the home may seem minor in comparison to a factory environment, factors such as the presence of children must be taken into account.

References and further reading

General duties, Health and Safety at Work etc Act 1974

Management of Health and Safety at Work Regulations 1999, SI 1999/3242
   (HMSO, London)

Human factors

'Human error' is an overworked phrase commonly cited to disguise a failure of a management system. It is often all too easy to point to someone's mistake as the cause of an accident. Many major accidents in recent years such as Flixborough, Bhopal, Chernobyl and Piper Alpha have been the result of human error, but the underlying or root causes have usually been found on investigation to lie in organisational weaknesses and systems failures which good management should have prevented.

'Human factors' is the expression coined to cover the organisational, job-related and personal factors that influence human behaviour. These factors can either add value through human intervention in a process, or can give rise to negative pressures that overstrain human reliability. 'Violation' is the term used by experts in this field to describe human behaviour which is against or in spite of 'the rules', and is the opposite of 'compliance'.

'Behavioural safety' is another term that crops up in this context. Some argue that understanding behaviour and the contribution of human errors and violations to workplace accidents enables organisations to improve safety culture. Trade unions sometimes describe this as a policy of 'blaming the worker' when things go wrong.

Nevertheless, human errors can be controlled by actively managing their causes. Issues to consider in the design of systems of work may include:

- fatigue
- shift work, long hours
- lone working
- organisational change
- training, competence
- communications
- alarm systems
- staffing levels, workload
- production pressures
- emergency procedures.

The Management Regulations apply and human factors need to be taken into account during risk assessment. Lessons need to be learnt from incident and near miss investigations, to enable preventive measures to be taken.

See also **Ergonomics**.

References and further reading

General duties, 1974 Act

Management of Health and Safety at Work Regulations 1999, SI 1999/3242
(HMSO, London)

HSE. *Reducing error and influencing behaviour*, HSG48 (HSE Books, Sudbury, 1999)

HSE. *Successful health and safety management*, HSG65 (HSE Books, Sudbury, 1997)

HSE. *Improving maintenance – a guide to reducing human error* (HSE Books,
Sudbury, 2000)

HSE report. *Fire at Hickson and Welch* (HSE Books, Sudbury, 1994)

HSE. *Organisational change and major accident hazards*, CHIS7 (HSE website,
www.hse.gov.uk)

Humidity

See **Environmental conditions**.

Infections

Infections at work can occur when workers are exposed to harmful micro-
organisms. These may be viruses, bacteria, fungi or internal parasites, and are
collectively covered by health and safety law as 'biological agents'. Several
thousand cases of hospital acquired infections (HAIs) are now believed to arise
every year.

Microbiologists who work with harmful micro-organisms are obviously at risk but
should usually be well aware of the special precautions to be taken. Farmers may be
exposed to zoonoses (animal-borne diseases that can be transmitted to humans) and
healthcare workers may accidentally become infected in the course of their work.
Cases of anthrax are rare but workers dealing with animal skins, wool and hair
from abroad may be at risk if these have not been properly disinfected.

In body piercing and tattoo parlours the public may be exposed to a risk of blood-borne viruses. Office workers may be exposed to Legionnaires' disease if cooling towers, eg for air conditioning systems, are poorly maintained. There have been a number of outbreaks in Britain in recent years from this cause. Wet cooling towers and evaporative condensers have to be notified to local authorities under regulations designed to control the spread of legionella bacteria.

The transport of dangerous goods, including micro-organisms, is covered by specific regulations concerned with the protection of everyone involved, directly or indirectly, with their transportation. Genetically modified organisms are also controlled under specific regulations. Exposure to most infections will generally be covered by the COSHH Regulations (see **Hazardous substances**), under the term 'biological agents', for which there is an 'Approved List'. Biological agents are classified into four hazard groups, the most hazardous of which may be handled only in laboratories with the highest standards of control.

Swine flu (H1N1) was declared a pandemic by the World Health Organization in June 2009 after the virus had spread from Mexico to many other countries. By the end of June, several thousand cases had occurred in the UK. The government has issued guidance to employers on precautions to be taken at work.

See also **Biological agents, Zoonoses.**

References and further reading

Carriage of Dangerous Goods and Use of Transportable Pressure Equipment Regulations 2004, SI 2004/568 (HMSO, London)

Control of Substances Hazardous to Health Regulations 2002, SI 2002/2677 (HMSO, London)

Department of Health. *Pandemic flu guidance for businesses* (DoH, 2009; www.dh.gov.uk)

Genetically Modified Organisms (Contained Use) Regulations 2000, SI 2000/2831 (HMSO, London)

HSE. *Anthrax – safe working and the prevention of infection*, HSG174 (HSE Books, Sudbury, 1997)

Notification of Cooling Towers and Evaporative Condensers Regulations 1992, SI 1992/2225 (HMSO, London)

Ionising radiations

See **Radiation**.

Joking

Joking or horseplay is part of working life but when taken too far can result in injury. Painting cracks on a grinding wheel may seem funny but when a real crack isn't spotted it may seriously injure someone when the wheel bursts. It may seem amusing to press an air-line against a fellow worker's anatomy but this is very dangerous.

Employers turn a blind eye to the more extreme forms of these antics at their peril and have a duty to do all that is reasonably practicable to prevent them. Employees have a duty under Section 7 of the 1974 Act not to endanger others, and face prosecution for offences.

References and further reading

Health and Safety at Work etc Act 1974, sections 2 and 7

Kitchens

The humble kitchen and canteen are well-loved features of many workplaces but can present a huge range of hazards, from scalding water and oil, knives and machinery, to gas, fire and even explosion. A serious fire occurred at Heathrow Airport when ventilation ducting containing accumulations of grease ignited.

Ventilation needs to be good and heat can be a problem. Food hygiene standards are inspected by environmental health officers, who also inspect for health and safety in the catering and hospitality industries. Risk assessments should not overlook the hazards in these areas. The HSE publishes numerous free advisory leaflets to assist employers in the catering industry.

References and further reading

HSE. *An index of health and safety guidance in the catering industry* (HSE website, www.hse.gov.uk)

Management of Health and Safety at Work Regulations 1999, SI 1999/3242 (HMSO, London)

Ladders

Ten ladder accidents on average are reported to the HSE every working day and these often involve serious or fatal injuries. Inappropriate use of stepladders is typically a factor. Attempts have been made to find practical solutions to replace ladders or help people to use them more safely. Overturning tower scaffolds are another problem. Previously, the law governing the use of ladders and other access equipment mainly consisted of the general duties in the 1974 Act, the Management Regulations requiring risk assessment, and the Construction (Health, Safety and Welfare) Regulations 1996 which require 'persons to be prevented from falling'.

However, a new European Directive, the Temporary Work at Heights Directive, has been implemented in Britain by new Work at Height Regulations.

Compliance with these regulations means that risk assessments must be carried out. Using ladders is not banned but will often be inappropriate. Other reasonably practicable alternatives must be found, such as podium steps and towers, trestles, scaffold cradles, gantries or mobile elevating work platforms or towers. Choice will depend on the situation and the findings of the risk assessment.

References and further reading

HSE. *The Work at Height Regulations 2005 – a brief guide* (HSE website, www.hse.gov.uk)

HSE. *Safe use of ladders and stepladders – an employer's guide* (HSE website, www.hse.gov.uk)

Management of Health and Safety at Work Regulations 1999, SI 1999/3242
    (HMSO, London)

Work at Height Regulations 2005, SI 2005/735 (HMSO, London)

Lead

Industrial lead poisoning was a common problem years ago but is rare these days. There are specific regulations for the control of exposure to lead.

While cases of acute poisoning are now unusual, lead absorption can still manifest itself and cause ill health if exposure to lead occurs, through absorption or ingestion, in activities such as stripping of old lead paint surfaces, plumbing, and lead acid battery manufacture.

The usual controls appropriate for hazardous substances are needed, including elimination of lead where possible, perhaps by substitution with less hazardous materials, containment of dust or fumes from processes, and extraction by exhaust ventilation, combined with the use of personal protective equipment and a high standard of welfare facilities.

Medical surveillance is important to monitor absorption and poisoning, particularly in pregnant workers.

Reference
Control of Lead at Work Regulations 2002, SI 2002/2676 (HMSO, London)

Legionnaires' disease
See **Infections**.

Lifting machinery
Operations involving lifting machinery are fraught with danger if the equipment used is unsuitable, poorly maintained or operated by incompetent people. Cranes collapse if overloaded and mobile cranes are particularly vulnerable to overturning if incorrectly set up. Safe working load indicators and alarms are needed to prevent mishaps from incorrect use. A host of slings, chains and ancillary equipment is involved and all needs to be subjected to a regime of periodic testing and examination by competent people, such as the specialist engineering inspectors of a company's insurance company.

As well as the usual duties under the 1974 Act and the Management Regulations, employers need to comply with specific regulations covering lifting machinery or operations.

References and further reading
General duties, Health and Safety at Work etc Act 1974

HSE. *A simple guide to the Lifting Operations and Lifting Equipment Regulations 1998*, INDG290 (HSE Books, Sudbury, 1998)

HSE. *Safe use of lifting equipment. Lifting Operations and Lifting Equipment Regulations 1998 – Approved Code of Practice and guidance*, L113 (HSE Books, Sudbury, 1998)

Lifting Operations and Lifting Equipment Regulations 1998 (LOLER), SI 1998/2307 (HMSO, London)

Management of Health and Safety at Work Regulations 1999, SI 1999/3242 (HMSO, London)

Lighting

See **Environmental conditions**.

Liquefied petroleum gas (LPG)

See **Gas**.

Long hours

Britain's so-called 'long hours' working culture has been blamed by some, including trade unions who are campaigning against the UK's opt-out from the EU Working Time Directive, to be the root cause of many accidents and cases of ill health, particularly stress-related ones. Be that as it may, there are legal requirements governing the minimum rest periods that workers, whether young people or adults, must be allowed. Employers need to take account of issues like fatigue, stress and morale when considering the effect that long hours and shift patterns may be having on the workforce, its morale and productivity.

See **Working time**.

References and further reading

Department of Trade and Industry. *Your guide to the Working Time Regulations* (DTI website, www.dti.gov.uk/er/work_time_regs/wtr0.htm)

Working Time Regulations 1998, SI 1998/1833 (HMSO, London)

Working Time (Amendment) Regulations 2003, SI 2003/1684 (HMSO, London)

Machinery

The European Machinery Directive (89/392/EEC) and subsequent amendments were implemented in Great Britain by regulations dealing with the supply of machinery, setting out procedures whereby machinery manufacturers must demonstrate conformity with certain 'essential health and safety requirements' (EHSRs). This enables the 'CE mark' to be applied to the machine. CE marked machinery can be traded across the EU. There is concern about the consistency of enforcement of these standards by member states and companies should be careful to make enquiries when ordering new equipment. The latest (third) amendment to the Directive seeks to simplify and clarify the procedures for demonstrating conformity with the standards.

Inadequate guarding (or fencing) of dangerous parts of machinery continues to be a cause of numerous serious injuries. Many technical solutions are available, such as fixed, interlocking or photoelectric guarding. Access to dangerous parts during maintenance can be protected by electrical interlocking, captive keys, lock-off systems and permits to work.

The comprehensive Provision and Use of Work Equipment Regulations ('PUWER') swept up many previous requirements to do with safety of machinery. The risk assessment requirements of the Management Regulations also apply.

References and further reading

European Commission. European Machinery Directive 89/392/EEC (*Official Journal of the European Communities*, 14 June 1989) and subsequent amendments

Management of Health and Safety at Work Regulations 1999, SI 1999/3242 (HMSO, London)

Provision and Use of Work Equipment Regulations 1998 (PUWER), SI 1998/2306 (HMSO, London)

Supply of Machinery (Safety) Regulations 1992, SI 1992/3073 (HMSO, London)

Supply of Machinery (Safety) (Amendment) Regulations 1994, SI 1994/2063 (HMSO, London)

Maintenance

Maintenance activities often have unnecessarily tragic outcomes. Access to machinery (often tempting the removal of guards for dangerous parts or unauthorised interference with safety devices), working at height, making repairs to electrical equipment and so on all present unusual hazards which are often uncontrolled because risk assessments are insufficient and systems of work are not well designed.

An HSE study of 326 deaths occurring during maintenance activities showed that 83 per cent of the accidents could have been eliminated completely by taking reasonably practicable precautions. Lives could have been saved in 70 per cent of the cases by positive management action. The most common causes of maintenance accidents were lack of adequate safe systems of work, failures to provide physical safeguards, poor management organisation, and inadequate information, instruction and training.

See also **Permits to work, Contractors**.

References and further reading

General duties, Health and Safety at Work etc Act 1974

Management of Health and Safety at Work Regulations 1999, SI 1999/3242 (HMSO, London)

HSE. *Deadly maintenance: a study of fatal accidents at work* (HMSO, London, 1985)

Manual handling

Over a third of all reportable (over three-day) injuries are caused by manual handling. Back injuries often occur through poor handling techniques, but hands, arms and feet are also frequently hurt. Every year 11 million working days are lost as a result, which costs employers £335 million.

As usual, employers have duties to assess risks and introduce safe methods of working. This will include training and supervision in appropriate lifting techniques. Introducing the mechanisation of manual handling tasks, where reasonably practicable, is often cost effective.

A tool for assessing risks from manual handling, 'Manual handling assessment chart' (MAC), has recently been developed by the HSE. Other such tools are also available.

References and further reading

General duties, Health and Safety at Work etc Act 1974

HSE. *Manual handling assessment chart (MAC) tool* (HSE website, www.hse.gov.uk/msd/mac)

Management of Health and Safety at Work Regulations 1999, SI 1999/3242
(HMSO, London)
Manual Handling Operations Regulations 1992, SI 1992/2793 (HMSO, London)

Mobile phones

Since December 2003 it has been an offence under road traffic legislation to use a hand-held phone while driving. Hands-free phones are not banned but it has been suggested that there might be a breach of health and safety law if an investigation showed that using the phone contributed to an accident. At the time of writing there is no case law to back this up.

Concern expressed about electromagnetic radiation risks has persuaded some individuals to use remote ear-pieces for their phones. Local public concern about the siting of mobile phone masts continues to arise in spite of assurances by scientists about safety.

See also **Driving.**

References and further reading
Department for Transport website, www.dft.gov.uk
General duties, Health and Safety at Work etc Act 1974
Management of Health and Safety at Work Regulations 1999, SI 1999/3242
(HMSO, London)
Road Traffic Acts 1988 and 1991
The Stationery Office. *The Highway Code* (TSO, London, 2007)

Nanotechnology

This is a relatively new technology involving the manufacture of very tiny things.

Concerns are being expressed in some quarters about the risk of inhalation and absorption into the body of tiny toxic particles. Fire and explosion risks may also exist. Little official guidance so far exists but the TUC has called for production and use of nanoparticles to be carried out in a contained process that protects workers from exposure.

In view of uncertainty about the risks involved in new technology of this kind, it is sensible to apply the 'precautionary principle', ie erring on the side of safety in applying risk control measures.

Reference

Management of Health and Safety at Work Regulations 1999, SI 1999/3242 (HMSO, London)

Noise

Noise at work is literally deafening. It is estimated that 170,000 people in the UK are suffering from deafness, tinnitus or other ear conditions caused by exposure to excessive noise at work.

While ageing results naturally in some hearing loss, particularly at higher frequencies, exposure to high noise levels exacerbates this condition. It can cause hearing damage and premature deafness over a range of frequencies in young as well as older workers, and lead to unpleasant conditions such as tinnitus. Damage to hearing is cumulative, whether caused outside or at work, and frequent or prolonged exposure to high noise levels will cause permanent, irreversible damage. Noise can also cause stress and interfere with communication which could be vital to safety.

What is a high level of noise, and what is regarded as acceptably safe? Noise is sometimes described as 'unwanted sound'. It is measured in decibels, usually represented as 'dB(A)'. If you find you are having to shout to communicate with someone a couple of metres away and cannot hear clearly what they are saying to you, the noise level, ie loudness or sound pressure, is likely to be around 85 dB(A). If you cannot hear at a distance of one metre, the level is likely to be around 90. Every increase of 3 dB(A) is a doubling of sound pressure. The most extreme levels of noise at work tend to be around 140 dB(A), which is like hearing a jet aircraft taking off 25 metres away.

The risk of suffering hearing damage depends not just on exposure to loud noise but on the duration of exposure. The total amount of noise exposure for individuals during the working day is called the 'daily personal noise exposure'. Employers are not obliged to provide an in-house audiometry service for employees but pre-employment and regular hearing checks for workers likely to be exposed to noise are wise.

Employers have a legal duty to reduce exposure to noise at work so far as is reasonably practicable. The Noise at Work Regulations 1989 implemented the relevant European Directive of 1986 in Britain. They required noise to be measured so that any necessary control measures could be taken. Measurement had to be done by someone competent to use the instruments and understand the results.

There are various engineering measures that can be taken to suppress noise. Obviously, installing less noisy machinery will help and there are now duties on manufacturers to design and construct quieter machinery and to supply noise data. Older, noisy machines can be enclosed with sound absorbing materials. Dampers and silencers can be fitted.

Management measures to reduce individuals' exposure could include job rotation and the provision of quiet refuges from where operators can control noisy processes. Personal hearing protection such as ear defenders may also need to be provided.

A new European Physical Agents (Noise) Directive has tightened the requirements. The Control of Noise at Work Regulations 2005, which came into force in 2006, have reduced the first two levels at which action must be taken from 85 and 90 to 80 and 85 dB(A). Health surveillance is required where there is a risk from exposure to noise. The limit of personal noise exposure is 87 dB(A).

This means that employers who have already taken action to control noise may have to do more, and some who did not have to do anything under the 1989 Regulations now have to.

See also **Vibration.**

References and further reading

Control of Noise at Work Regulations 2005, SI 2005/1643 (HMSO, London)

HSE, free leaflet. *Noise at work: advice for employers*, INDG362 (HSE Books, Sudbury, 2002)

HSE, free leaflet. *Proposals for new Control of Noise at Work Regulations implementing the Physical Agents (Noise) Directive (2003/10/EC)* (HSE Books, Sudbury)

HSE. *Protect your hearing or lose it!*, INDG363 (HSE Books, Sudbury, 2002)

HSE. *Controlling noise at work. The Control of Noise at Work Regulations 2005. Guidance on Regulations*, L108 (HSE Books, Sudbury, 2005)

HSE. *Sound solutions: techniques to reduce noise at work*, HSG138 (HSE Books, Sudbury, 1995)

Non-ionising radiation

See **Radiation**.

Offices

More people than ever are employed these days in offices. Risks to their health and safety may seem much less severe than in, say, the harsh environments of the construction or agricultural sectors, and that is generally true. But this should not allow complacency. The same general duties to ensure the health and safety of employees apply, and proper risk assessments will often reveal numerous hazards confronting office workers, some of them serious. These may include poor environmental conditions, overcrowding, electrical and machinery hazards, fire risks, exposure to fumes, eye strain from working with VDUs, musculoskeletal problems from working at poorly designed workstations, and stress.

References and further reading

General duties, Health and Safety at Work etc Act 1974

HSE. *Offices, Shops and Railway Premises Act 1963*, OSR1 (HSE Books, Sudbury, 1994)

HSE, free leaflet. *Officewise*, INDG173 (HSE website, www.hse.gov.uk/pubns/indg173.pdf)

Management of Health and Safety at Work Regulations 1999, SI 1999/3242 (HMSO, London)

Workplace (Health, Safety and Welfare) Regulations 1992, SI 1992/3004 (HMSO, London)

Overcrowding

Overcrowding can be unpleasant, unhealthy and even unsafe. The minimum space requirements that used to be contained in law, 40 square feet of floor space and 400 cubic feet per person, were intended to avoid this. While today the HSE recommends 11 cubic metres per person, the risk assessment requirements of the Management Regulations and the Workplace Regulations mean that each case needs to be looked at on its own merits. 'Sufficient' floor area, height and unoccupied space are factors that need to be considered in achieving decent working conditions.

References and further reading

General duties, Health and Safety at Work etc Act 1974

HSE. *Essentials of health and safety at work* (HSE Books, Sudbury, 2003)

HSE, free leaflet. *Officewise*, INDG173 (HSE website, www.hse.gov.uk/pubns/indg173.pdf)

Management of Health and Safety at Work Regulations 1999, SI 1999/3242 (HMSO, London)

Workplace (Health, Safety and Welfare) Regulations 1992, SI 1992/3004 (HMSO, London)

Passive smoking

See **Smoking**.

Permits to work

A 'permit to work' is the expression given to a written authorisation to carry out work in potentially hazardous situations, eg welding in a confined space where there could be flammable or toxic residues. The permit will specify conditions which will have been set as a result of a risk assessment and may describe working methods in detail. They are a valuable element of safe working systems, particularly in high-hazard industries where there is a need for frequent maintenance without total shutdown. A system will be required to manage the paperwork associated with the authorisations.

See also **Confined spaces**.

References and further reading

Management of Health and Safety at Work Regulations 1999, SI 1999/3242
    (HMSO, London)

Work in Confined Spaces Regulations 1997, SI 1997/1713 (HMSO, London)

Personal protective equipment (PPE)

The term 'personal protective equipment' or 'PPE' covers a wide range of protection for workers against a variety of hazards. Depending on what these are, hard hats, eye protection, gloves, boots, overalls and respirators including self contained breathing apparatus may be appropriate.

Hard hats need to be worn wherever there is risk of being struck by a falling object and it is usually sensible to wear safety shoes or boots in factories or sites where there is a risk of feet being crushed or stepping on sharp objects.

It will often be possible to eliminate exposure to a hazard, for example a toxic substance, by substituting a less hazardous one, by containing the process and by exhaust ventilation. However, in some circumstances this will not always be sufficient. The appropriate PPE should be supplied, kept clean and in good condition and renewed when necessary. Wearing of PPE in circumstances where this is vital to the protection of workers' health and safety should be properly supervised.

References and further reading

Construction (Design and Management) Regulations 2007, SI 2007/320 (HMSO,
    London)

Control of Substances Hazardous to Health Regulations 2002, SI 2002/2677 (HMSO, London)

Control of Substances Hazardous to Health (Amendment) Regulations 2004, SI 2004/3386 (HMSO, London)

Personal Protective Equipment at Work Regulations 1992, SI 1992/2966 (HMSO, London)

Management of Health and Safety at Work Regulations 1999, SI 1999/3242 (HMSO, London)

Pregnancy

Government statistics suggest that 350,000 pregnant women per annum are at work and 240,000 per annum return to work after giving birth. More than one in four pregnant women experience a miscarriage, one in 200 babies is stillborn, and one in 100 is premature.

The Equal Opportunities Commission found in 2001 that out of 1,434 potential tribunal cases involving pregnancy or maternity-related discrimination, 1,387 involved a breach of health and safety law. The average award for dismissal due to pregnancy is around £10,000. The DTI estimates that it costs firms £3,500 per employee to recruit staff after a new or expectant mother has left.

Employers have a duty under health and safety law to protect women of childbearing age from hazards and risks in the workplace. In particular, the Management of Health and Safety at Work Regulations apply and the HSE has published guidance on how to carry out a risk assessment to identify potential hazards and the possible chemical, physical and biological risks for pregnant workers. For example, new and expectant mothers should not:

- lift or carry heavy loads
- work long hours
- stand or sit for long periods of time
- work in noisy, stressful or violent environments
- work at unsuitable workstations
- work with lead
- be exposed to infectious diseases.

References and further reading

General duties, Health and Safety at Work etc Act 1974

HSE. *New and expectant mothers at work: a guide for employers*, HSG122 (HSE Books, Sudbury, 2002)

Management of Health and Safety at Work Regulations 1999, SI 1999/3242 (HMSO, London)

Pressure systems

About 150 incidents occur every year involving pressure systems. These include steam plant, air compressors and receivers, autoclaves, reaction vessels, gas and hydraulic storage tanks and the valves and pipework associated with all of these.

Failure of a pressure vessel such as a steam boiler or air receiver is bad enough, but the consequences can be far worse if it contains toxic or flammable substances, particularly if these have been heated. Failure of a pressure system can have catastrophic results. One of the most dramatic failures in the UK in recent memory was the cyclohexane explosion at a chemical plant in Flixborough, Lincolnshire, in 1974 which killed 28 people after a temporary bellows in pipework failed. The rupture of an LPG sphere in an oil refinery at Feyzin,

France, in 1966 allowed a gas cloud to roll over the adjacent motorway where it caught fire and engulfed a number of passing vehicles.

There are regulations specific to these risks, contained in the Pressure Systems Safety Regulations 2000. These require all pressurised plant and systems to be designed, constructed and installed to prevent danger and to have safety devices; systems must be properly maintained; any repairs and modifications must not cause danger; a competent person must prepare a written scheme for examination of the plant; the plant must be examined and records must be kept. Plant must, of course, be operated safely.

It used to be the case that periods were prescribed for regular examination, such as every 14 months for steam boilers, but this is now left to the judgment of the competent person drawing up the written scheme of examination. Information about competent persons' organisations is available from the United Kingdom Accreditation Service (UKAS) (see reference below).

References and further reading

Carriage of Dangerous Goods and Use of Transportable Pressure Equipment Regulations 2004, SI 2004/568 (HMSO, London)

HSE. *Safety of pressure systems. Pressure Systems Safety Regulations 2000 – Approved Code of Practice*, L122 (HSE Books, Sudbury, 2000)

Pressure Equipment Regulations 1999, SI 1999/2001 (HMSO, London)

Pressure Systems Safety Regulations 2000, SI 2000/128 (HMSO, London)

Simple Pressure Vessel (Safety) Regulations 1991 (as amended), SI 1991/2749 (HMSO, London)

UKAS, 21–47 High Street, Feltham, Middlesex TW13 4UN

Public safety

Companies are required to conduct their undertaking so as to ensure the health and safety not only of their own employees but of others, including members of the public, who may be affected by work activities (Section 3, 1974 Act). This will include visitors, casual passers-by and nearby residents, all of whom are entitled to protection from risks arising from the conduct of the undertaking. Major hazard sites, where there could be off-site risks in the event of a catastrophe, must prepare emergency plans in collaboration with local authorities. Quarries and other sites where trespassing is foreseen need to take steps to prevent access. For construction work, other legislation lays down specific safety requirements for work in the street.

References and further reading

HSE. *Health and safety regulation: a short guide*, HSC13 (HSE website, www.hse.gov.uk/pubns/hsc13.pdf)

HSE. *Protecting the public – your next move*, HSG151 (HSE Books, Sudbury, 1997)

New Roads and Street Works Act 1991

Control of Major Accident Hazards Regulations 1999, SI 1999/743 (HMSO, London)

Quality

Much has been written about the value of integrating the management of health and safety with other management systems, including those for the environment and quality. These systems share broadly similar principles and in larger companies are increasingly seen as coming under the charge of a single manager or department. There is no legal compulsion to go down this route but for some companies it may bring benefits of consistency and cost effectiveness.

References and further reading

Institution of Occupational Safety and Health, free document. *Joined-up working: an introduction to integrated management systems* (IOSH, Leicester, 2006)

International Organization for Standardization. ISO 9000 and ISO 14000

Radiation

Radiation may be ionising or non-ionising, and both forms can be harmful to health. Everyone is exposed to some natural background radiation. Ionising radiation occurs naturally (eg in the form of radon gas) and can also be produced artificially. It occurs either in the form of electromagnetic rays such as X-rays and gamma rays, or particles such as alpha and beta particles. It may be used in medicine, either for diagnosis or treatment, in industry for measurement and testing and for electricity generation, and in research and teaching.

Non-ionising radiation is either optical, eg ultraviolet (UV) radiation from the sun, which may cause skin cancer, and from lasers, which can cause burns and damage the eyes, or it arises from electromagnetic fields, eg microwaves and radio frequencies.

The Ionising Radiations Regulations (IRR) cover the use of sealed and unsealed radioactive sources such as those found in medical equipment, X-ray sets, radiography or measurement devices.

References and further reading

HSE. *Work with ionising radiation. Ionising Radiations Regulations 1999 Approved Code of Practice and guidance*, L121 (HSE Books, Sudbury, 2000)

Ionising Radiations Regulations 1999, SI 1999/3232 (HMSO, London)

Management of Health and Safety at Work Regulations 1999, SI 1999/3242 (HMSO, London)

Repetitive strain injury

Repetitive strain injuries (RSIs) were famously pronounced by one judge as not to exist as a condition of occupational ill health but this opinion has been discredited. Well-known conditions such as writer's cramp existed long before this modern term was invented for pains and loss of muscular control caused by repetitive work with arms and hands. Many different groups of workers employed on tasks requiring repetitive muscle and tendon movement, such as keyboard operators and checkout staff at supermarkets, are at risk.

See also **Ergonomics**.

References and further reading

HSE. *A pain in your workplace? Ergonomic problems and solutions*, HSG121 (HSE Books, Sudbury, 1994)

Manual Handling Operations Regulations 1992, SI 1992/2793 (HMSO, London)

Respiratory protective equipment (RPE)

Dust, mist and fumes are produced by processes like grinding, spraying and welding. Gases and vapours may also be released into the workplace atmosphere. Where these are hazardous to health (they may usually be assumed to be so) and cannot be effectively controlled by local ventilation such as fans, hoods and ducts or fume cupboards, suitable respiratory protective equipment must be provided.

The COSHH Regulations require employers to carry out assessments of risks of employees' exposure to substances liable to injure their health.

References and further reading

Control of Substances Hazardous to Health Regulations 2002, SI 2002/2677 (HMSO, London)

Control of Substances Hazardous to Health (Amendment) Regulations 2005, SI 2005/3386 (HMSO, London)

HSE, free leaflet. *A short guide to the Personal Protective Equipment at Work Regulations 1992*, INDG174 (HSE Books, Sudbury, 1995)

HSE. *The selection, use and maintenance of respiratory protective equipment*, HSG53 (HSE Books, Sudbury, 2004)

Personal Protective Equipment at Work Regulations 1992, SI 1992/2966 (HMSO, London)

Respiratory sensitisers

Respiratory sensitisers are substances which can cause an allergic reaction in the respiratory system, sometimes asthma. Typically, occupational diseases such as farmer's lung are caused by these substances.

See **Asthma**.

Sick building syndrome

Sick building syndrome is a term used to describe the troublesome range of cold or flu-like symptoms that are exhibited by numerous occupants of some buildings. It has been recognised by the World Health Organisation since 1982. There is no single cause but often affected buildings are new or have been recently refurbished.

The problem can usually be overcome by actions such as improving ventilation, overhauling air conditioning systems, reviewing the use of any chemicals, installing better lighting, better cleaning, and replacing any fume-emitting equipment.

See also **Environmental conditions.**

References and further reading

General duties, Health and Safety at Work etc Act 1974

HSE. *How to deal with sick building syndrome – guidance for employers, building owners and building managers*, HSG132 (HSE Books, Sudbury, 1995)

Management of Health and Safety at Work Regulations 1999, SI 1999/3242 (HMSO, London)

Workplace (Health, Safety and Welfare) Regulations 1992, SI 1992/3004 (HMSO, London)

Skin disease

See **Dermatitis.**

Slips, trips and falls

Slips, trips and falls on the level are the most common cause of major injuries and one of the main causes of over three-day absences. One occurs every three minutes, accounting for one-third of all reported major injuries, 20 per cent of over three-day injuries to employees and 50 per cent of all reported accidents to members of the public. They cost employers £512 million a year and society £918 million. Slips, trips and falls have therefore been targeted for reduction in order to help achieve the government's national target of a 30 per cent reduction in injuries by 2010.

Hazards include slippery floor surfaces, contamination by grease and oil, holes in gangways, floors, pot holes, trailing cables, cluttered working spaces, obstructed gangways and the like.

Precautions are basic good housekeeping, maintenance of floors, gangways, corridors and stairs, prevention of spillages and contamination, keeping gangways and working areas clear, provision of non-slip surfaces where appropriate and regular maintenance of areas and roadways subject to hard wear and tear. Adequate lighting should be provided.

See also **Falls from height**.

References and further reading

HSE, free leaflet. *Preventing slips, trips and falls at work*, INDG225 (HSE Books, Sudbury, 2003)

HSE. *Slips and trips: guidance for employers on identifying hazards and controlling risks*, HSG155 (HSE Books, Sudbury, 1996)

Workplace (Health, Safety and Welfare) Regulations 1992, SI 1992/3004 (HMSO, London)

Smoking

Smoking, including passive smoking, is known to damage health and cause fires but just how best to control these risks remains controversial. Some countries such as Ireland and Norway have already introduced bans on smoking in the workplace, including public bars and restaurants, while the UK is in the process of doing so. Smoking was banned on the London Underground after it was believed to have caused the King's Cross fire.

The general duties in the 1974 Act, the Management of Health and Safety at Work Regulations 1999 and the Workplace (Health, Safety and Welfare) Regulations 1992 control risks associated with smoking in the workplace. A consultation document was issued in 2005, but there is not yet an approved code of practice.

Employers are advised to introduce a policy on passive smoking in consultation with their employees, regard non-smoking as the norm in enclosed places, segregate smokers from non-smokers and take steps in rest rooms and areas to protect non-smokers from discomfort caused by tobacco smoke.

Smoking in enclosed public places was banned in the Republic of Ireland in 2004. Scotland followed in 2006 and England, Wales and Northern Ireland enacted similar legislation in 2007.

References and further reading

Workplace (Health, Safety and Welfare) Regulations 1992, SI 1992/3004 (HMSO, London)

Management of Health and Safety at Work Regulations 1999, SI 1999/3242 (HMSO, London)

HSE, free leaflet. *Passive smoking at work*, INDG63 (HSE Books, Sudbury, 1997)

Prohibition of Smoking in Certain Premises (Scotland) Regulations 2006, SSI 2006/90 (Scottish Executive, Edinburgh)

Smoke-free (Premises and Enforcement) Regulations 2006, SI 2006/3368 (HMSO, London)

Smoke-free Premises etc. (Wales) Regulations 2007, SI 2007/787 (W.68) (National Assembly for Wales, Cardiff)

Smoking (Northern Ireland) Order 2006, SI 2006/2957 (N.I.20) (HMSO, London)

The Stationery Office, White Paper. *Smoking kills* (TSO, London)

Stress

Up to 5 million workers in the UK were reported in a 1995 survey to feel 'very' or 'extremely' stressed by their work and of those around half a million believed they suffered from stress that was making them ill, and that it was caused by work. Stress was estimated then to cost the UK about £3.7 billion a year.

A survey by the European Foundation published in 1996 reported that 28 per cent of workers across the European Union suffered stress-related health problems.

Stress at work causes a great deal of absence and is hugely damaging to productivity. The EU estimates that 41 million working days are lost from this cause each year out of a total of 600 million due to all causes of work-related ill health.

Stress is undeniably a health issue and employers have responsibilities for protecting the health of their workers under the 1974 Act and the Management of Health and Safety Regulations. In today's litigious society with its compensation culture it is likely that civil actions for stress-related cases will follow if companies are unable to show that they are taking all reasonably practicable steps to manage the problem.

What exactly is the problem? The HSE defines stress as 'the adverse reaction people have to excessive pressure or other demands placed on them'. Whereas perhaps as little as 20 years ago stress was hardly recognised as an occupational hazard, society's expectations and factors in the modern working environment have changed since then. The workplace now includes a growing number of older workers, teleworking, increased use of information and communication technology, greater demands for working flexibly with multiple skills and multifunctional working, often in teams. More and more people work in the services sector and in places such as call centres.

Not all forms of stress are necessarily bad. Stress derives from our primitive survival instincts of 'fight or flight' which occur in response to stimulants that experts like to call 'stressors'. Stressors are demands that tax the individual's capacity to the limit or beyond. Some stress is positive and some people will voluntarily accept experiencing quite extreme risks for the sheer thrill of the adrenalin rush: witness the popularity of bungee jumping.

However, the stressors causing work-related problems are often negative in their effect. Examples include having to work to very tight deadlines, at very high speeds or on boring or monotonous tasks, with little or no influence or control over the task by the individual. Some blame the UK's 'long hours culture', others blame the introduction of business efficiency methods such as outsourcing, subcontracting, downsizing (or 'right sizing') and the pressures of globalisation and greater insecurity of employment.

Whatever the causes, the problem seems to be worsening. In 2002 the HSE published figures showing that twice as many workers were reporting stress than in 1990. Stress, which some experts are calling a 'psychosocial disease', is now second only to back pain as a cause of time off work. It can also cause tension in the workplace, leading to bullying and other forms of antisocial behaviour. Experts are unfortunately eager to point out that it is not easy to separate work-related stressors from related problems in the wider society such as social inequality, diversity, race, gender, disability and age.

Many employers now have to bear the high costs of loss of productivity from absenteeism, or even 'presenteeism', a term used by some experts to describe the phenomenon of employees feeling under pressure to come in to work but being unable to concentrate on their tasks because they have been working excessive hours, or are ill or suffering from stress. And growing awareness of the success of recent claims for damages for stress-related illness caused by work is likely to encourage individuals to pursue compensation cases, with help from firms of specialist lawyers or with the backing of their trade union.

How is stress to be managed? Some managers may be so intimidated by the magnitude of the problem as to think that there is little or nothing they can do to manage it. There is in fact a great deal known about how to manage stress. Research has found that it can be successfully managed in the same way as other health and safety issues, using the same management model (see Part 1 of this book). Risk assessments should include paying attention to any stressors that may be occurring in the company. Analysis of sickness or absence records can help identify what these might be. Significant findings should be recorded.

What preventive measures are likely to succeed? Research has shown that the problem of work-related stress derives from poor design, organisation and management of work. Stress is experienced when the demands of work exceed the ability to cope or to control the situation. Understanding this helps managers to focus attention on the work-related causes and introduce appropriate preventive measures, such as redesigning the job. This will often lead to worthwhile productivity improvements. Stress awareness training for managers can also help.

The HSE has recently published Management Standards for work-related stress, which are intended to enable managers to gauge stress levels, identify causes and work with employees to resolve issues.

References and further reading

European Agency for Safety and Health at Work. *Guidance on work-related stress: spice of life or kiss of death?*, N22-EN (European Commission, Luxembourg, 2001; on the Internet at agency.osha.eu.int/publications/factsheets/22/en/ FACTSHEETSN22_EN.PDF)

European Commission, Green Paper. *Promoting a European framework for corporate social responsibility* (European Commission, 2001)

European Standard EN ISO 10075-1 and 2: Ergonomic principles related to mental workload

General duties, Health and Safety at Work etc Act 1974

HSE. *Management standards for work-related stress* (HSE website, www.hse.gov.uk/stress/standards)

Management of Health and Safety at Work Regulations 1999, SI 1999/3242 (HMSO, London)

Transport

Not counting road-related incidents, about 70 people a year are killed in accidents involving vehicles at work. Works transport accidents are the second biggest cause of fatal injuries at work and also account for 1,000 major injuries a year.

Being struck by a moving vehicle is the principal cause of injury, often during reversing operations. Vehicles overturning, unsecured loads and people simply falling off vehicles are other common causes. Brake and steering failures are often involved.

As always, risk assessment is the key to controlling transport hazards. Sites, vehicles and drivers are the three main elements which need to be covered by a risk control management system. It is essential to segregate vehicles and pedestrians and ensure that vehicles reverse safely. Vehicles should be properly maintained and driven only by authorised personnel.

See also **Driving** and **Forklift trucks**

References and further reading

Construction (Design and Management) Regulations 2007, SI 2007/320 (HMSO, London)

HSE, free leaflet. *Managing vehicle safety at the workplace: a short guide for employers*, INDG199 (HSE Books, Sudbury, 1995)

HSE. *Workplace transport safety – guidance for employers*, HSG136 (HSE Books, Sudbury, 1995)

Management of Health and Safety at Work Regulations 1999, SI 1999/3242 (HMSO, London)

Provision and Use of Work Equipment Regulations 1998, SI 1998/2306 (HMSO, London)

Workplace (Health, Safety and Welfare) Regulations 1992, SI 1992/3004 (HMSO, London)

Underground rooms

Underground rooms or basements used as workrooms can present problems. Ventilation needs to be good, lighting and ceiling height must be adequate and two routes to safety are needed in the event of fire. It is plainly unwise to run a process with high fire risks in a basement, but it is surprising how often this occurs. Depending on circumstances, an inspector may well decide to serve a prohibition notice.

References and further reading

Management of Health and Safety at Work Regulations 1999, SI 1999/3242 (HMSO, London)

Workplace (Health, Safety and Welfare) Regulations 1992, SI 1992/3004 (HMSO, London)

Vehicles

See **Transport**.

Vibration

Injury from vibration, particularly of the hand or arm, can be caused by machinery or powered hand-tools. 'Hand–arm vibration syndrome' (HAVS) is a term used for a painful and irreversible condition which includes 'vibration white finger'.

Vibration can also affect the whole body, for example by causing back problems when vibration from a machine or vehicle passes through the seat to the driver's body ('whole body vibration' or WBV).

Vibration is specifically controlled under the European Physical Agents (Vibration) Directive and was implemented in Great Britain by the Control of Vibration at Work Regulations 2005. Suppliers of machinery have a duty to reduce risks to a minimum and provide data on vibration.

References and further reading

Control of Vibration at Work Regulations 2005, SI 2005/1093 (HMSO, London)

European Commission. Physical Agents (Vibration) Directive 2002/44/EC (*Official Journal of the European Communities*, 25 June 2002)

HSE. *Hand–arm vibration*, HSG88 (HSE Books, Sudbury, 1994)

HSE. *Vibration solutions: practical ways to reduce the risk of hand–arm vibration injury*, HSG170 (HSE Books, Sudbury, 1997)

Management of Health and Safety at Work Regulations 1999, SI 1999/3242 (HMSO, London)

Provision and Use of Work Equipment Regulations 1998, SI 1998/2306 (HMSO, London)

Supply of Machinery (Safety) Regulations 1992, SI 1992/3073 (HMSO, London)

Supply of Machinery (Safety) (Amendment) Regulations 1994, SI 1994/2063 (HMSO, London)

Violence

The HSE defines work-related violence as 'any incident in which an employee is abused, threatened or assaulted in circumstances relevant to their work'.

Violence towards employees, which includes bullying behaviour, generally arises from either members of the public or from other employees. Lone workers, including those who have to visit private premises or work at night, are especially vulnerable.

Work-related violence is a significant safety risk today, particularly for certain occupational categories such as nurses, security personnel, drivers, police and prison staff, shop attendants, social workers and others in public services who may face anger or be at risk of robbery with violence. Statistics published in the British Crime Survey for 2006/07 estimate the number of incidents of violence at work, including threats as well as physical assaults, at 685,000. The peak appears to have been in 1995 when 1,310,000 incidents are believed to have occurred. Even so, the latest figures remain unacceptably high.

Risk assessments under the Management of Health and Safety at Work Regulations should include consideration of the risk of violence to staff. Depending on the nature of the risks identified, preventive measures may be needed to protect workers, such as organisational changes, physical modification to premises, introduction of security routines, use of technical aids, information and training.

Employees should be able to get prompt assistance in the event of attack and this should be anticipated in the preparation of an action plan, which should be rehearsed from time to time. If the worst happens and in spite of these precautions workers are attacked, full and prompt collaboration by employers with the police to secure convictions of aggressors will be essential to restore morale and demonstrate the company's determination to protect its employees. Victim support is also important.

Under the Reporting of Injuries, Diseases and Dangerous Occurrences Regulations 1995 (RIDDOR), an incident of physical violence to an employee should be reported if it results in more than three days off work.

The Sex Discrimination Act 1975 and the Race Relations Act 1976 cover cases of verbal abuse and are enforced by the Equal Opportunities Commission and the Commission for Racial Equality. The Public Order Act 1986 is enforced by the police against threats, abuse and physical assaults but only applies after an offence has been committed.

The HSE's guidance for employers for dealing with violence sets out a four-stage approach:

- find out if you have a problem
- decide what action to take
- take action
- check what you have done.

It is a good idea to involve employees in developing a company policy for preventing violence. The HSE has also published specific guidance on violence and aggression to staff in the health services and in education.

References and further reading

HSE, free leaflet. *Violence at work: a guide for employers*, INDG69 (HSE Books, Sudbury, 1996)

HSE. *Violence at work: findings from the 2002/03 British Crime Survey* (HSE website, www.hse.gov.uk)

Management of Health and Safety at Work Regulations 1999, SI 1999/3242 (HMSO, London)

The Suzy Lamplugh Trust, www.suzylamplugh.org

Welfare

The welfare provisions of the 1974 Act and associated regulations should not be overlooked. Decent standards of welfare facilities, including lavatories, washrooms, places to store and consume food and drink, and rest areas, are expected by employees and standards are set down in the law.

References and further reading

HSE. *Essentials of health and safety at work* (HSE Books, Sudbury, 2003)

Workplace (Health, Safety and Welfare) Regulations 1992, SI 1992/3004 (HMSO, London)

Whistle-blowing

There is protection under the Public Interest Disclosure Act for employees who blow the whistle on criminal activities, which may include breaches of health and safety law. It is better for a company to establish a culture in which employees do not fear victimisation if they bring to the management's attention matters that concern them. Often a safety committee that is working well and is therefore trusted by the workforce will be the best place for issues to be addressed.

Reference

The Public Interest Disclosure Act 1998

Work equipment

The term 'work equipment' covers a wide spectrum from heavy machinery to hand tools and other articles forming the paraphernalia of work activities. Various existing legal requirements were swept up by the Provision and Use of Work Equipment Regulations and, as usual, the risk assessment requirements of the Management Regulations also apply.

Electricity, lifting equipment and hazardous substances are dealt with under other specific regulations.

References and further reading

HSE. *Essentials of health and safety at work* (HSE Books, Sudbury, 2003)

Management of Health and Safety at Work Regulations 1999, SI 1999/3242 (HMSO, London)

Provision and Use of Work Equipment Regulations 1998 ('PUWER'), SI 1998/2306 (HMSO, London)

Working time

Working time is the subject of a European Directive from which Britain has secured a controversial opt-out allowing employees to work more than 48 hours a week voluntarily.

The Working Time Regulations 1998 require that workers should have:

- an average working limit of 48 hours a week
- an uninterrupted break of 20 minutes when daily working time exceeds six hours (though not if there is a need for continuity of service or production or a foreseeable surge in activity)
- a rest period of 11 consecutive hours in every 24 hours
- one day off a week, averaged over two weeks
- an 8 hours in 24 (average) working limit for night workers
- free health assessments for night work
- four weeks' paid annual leave.

Young or adolescent workers are entitled to a break of 30 minutes if they are required to work more than four and a half hours at a time, and 12 hours' rest in every 24. They are also entitled to two days off per week (this may not be averaged over two weeks).

The regulations were amended in 2003 to cover all non-mobile workers in road, sea, inland waterways and lake transport, all workers in the railways and offshore industries, and all workers in aviation who are not covered by the Civil Aviation Working Time Regulations. Junior doctors were included in 2004 and should not work more than 58 hours.

Advice and guidance is available from the Advisory, Conciliation and Arbitration Service (ACAS) and the Department of Trade and Industry. Enforcement is shared, depending on the industry, between the HSE, the Civil Aviation Authority, the Vehicle and Operator Services Agency and the Maritime and Coastguard Agency.

References and further reading

Department of Health. *Guidance for doctors in training* (Department of Health website, www.dh.gov.uk)

Department for Business Enterprise and Regulatory Reform. *Working Time Regulations* (www.berr.gov.uk/whatwedo/employment/working-time-regs/index.html)

European Commission. Working Time Directive, 93/104/EC (*Official Journal of the European Communities*, 23 November 1993)

Working Time Regulations 1998, SI 1998/1833 (HMSO, London)

Working Time (Amendment) Regulations 2003, SI 2003/1684 (HMSO, London)

Work-related upper limb disorders

Work-related upper limb disorders (WRULDs) are a form of musculoskeletal disorder caused by repeated or excessive physical effort. They are very common and a major cause of lost working time. Risk assessments leading to good design of tasks, training in safe lifting techniques, better layout of work stations and the like can reduce the incidence of WRULDs.

See **Ergonomics**.

References and further reading

General duties, Health and Safety at Work etc Act 1974

HSE. *A pain in your workplace? ergonomic problems and solutions*, HSG121 (HSE Books, Sudbury, 1994)

Management of Health and Safety at Work Regulations 1999, SI 1999/3242 (HMSO, London)

X-rays

X-ray equipment is commonly used in industry for non-destructive testing and examinations, in dentistry and for medical purposes. Use of X-ray equipment is safe provided that the equipment is properly maintained and used by a competent operator. It has sometimes been found that faulty equipment believed to be switched off has unwittingly remained on, exposing workers or patients to an excessive dose.

The Ionising Radiations Regulations set out detailed requirements for controlling radiation risks. See **Radiation**.

Reference

Ionising Radiations Regulations 1999, SI 1999/3232 (HMSO, London)

Young persons

Under the Health and Safety (Young Persons) Regulations certain restrictions are placed on what young people under 18 years of age may do.

Young people, particularly school leavers, are inexperienced about risks at work and especially vulnerable when they have just begun working. There are tragic examples of fatal accidents to teenagers in their first week at work. The courts are hard on employers who expose young people to needless risk.

Effective induction training and supervision is vital. Some tasks are simply too hazardous for young people to be left to do unsupervised, even if they have been trained. They tend to be enthusiastic and keen to show their worth, and easily overreach themselves in terms of their capability and knowledge of risks.

Risk assessments must take account of these factors. It may be a good idea for an older, experienced worker to mentor a new starter. It is, of course, the employer's duty to ensure their health and safety.

There are certain restrictions on young persons' hours of work. See also **Children, Working time.**

References and further reading

Activity Centres (Young Persons' Safety) Act 1995

General duties, Health and Safety at Work etc Act 1974

Health and Safety (Young Persons) Regulations 1997, SI 1997/135 (HMSO, London)

HSE. *Young people at work – a guide for employers*, HSG165 (HSE Books, Sudbury, 2000)

Management of Health and Safety at Work Regulations 1999, SI 1999/3242 (HMSO, London)

Zoonoses

Zoonoses are diseases transferred from animals to humans. It is estimated that some 300,000 workers in a variety of occupations are exposed to about 40 potential zoonoses in the UK. Most infections tend to be mild and self-limiting but some can be acute and cause long term health effects.

See **Infections.**

References and further reading

Control of Substances Hazardous to Health Regulations 2002, SI 2002/2677 (HMSO, London)

Control of Substances Hazardous to Health (Amendment) Regulations 2004, SI
2004/3386 (HMSO, London)
Management of Health and Safety at Work Regulations 1999, SI 1999/3242
(HMSO, London)

Part 3
Headline facts and figures

Disasters and catastrophes

Hindsight sees only too clearly how disasters might have been avoided. There is often something useful to be learned from them. Political reaction includes tightening regulations and establishing new regulatory authorities for licensing high-hazard activities.

Here are just a score or so of the numerous catastrophes that have occurred in recent times and the lessons learned, sometimes at severe cost to a company's reputation.

Aberfan, Wales, 1966

After two days of heavy rain a tip of spoil from a coal mine slid down a hillside into the mining village of Aberfan, destroying in its path a farm cottage and its occupants and engulfing the junior school and nearby houses. Although the tip operators saw the slide begin they were unable to raise the alarm because their telephone was out of action, though it is unlikely that any warning could have been given in time to help the victims. One hundred and forty-four people died, including 116 schoolchildren.

The National Coal Board was criticised severely by the Tribunal of Inquiry for failing to control the stability of the tip, which had been undermined by a spring. The Mines and Quarries (Tips) Act 1969 was then passed, requiring safe management of the hazard from tips.

Feyzin, France, 1966

A cloud of gas escaped from a propane storage sphere at the Feyzin refinery adjacent to the A6 autoroute near Lyon during an operation to drain off an aqueous layer from the sphere. A blockage caused by ice had occurred when a valve was opened, and when it suddenly freed itself propane gushed out of the sphere uncontrolled, drifting across the autoroute. Passing traffic was stopped but the gas cloud is believed to have been ignited nevertheless by a car. The sphere became engulfed in flames.

Firefighters attended but were inexperienced in dealing with such a fire and failed to cool the gas storage spheres. The first burst, toppling another, and altogether five were destroyed in the ensuing fires. Eighteen people were killed and 81 more were injured.

The incident raised a number of questions about the design and operation of the spheres, the lack of insulation to prevent icing, the lack of drainage to a bunded area where the LPG might have burned harmlessly, delays in activating emergency procedures and flaws in emergency planning. Lessons learned for design and operating procedures were subsequently incorporated into industry codes of practice.

Flixborough, England, 1974

Twenty-eight workers were killed, a further 36 suffered injuries and the plant was totally destroyed when a temporary bypass ruptured in a pressurised chemical processing system containing heated cyclohexane, a flammable liquid, resulting in a massive explosion and fires. A further 53 people were injured off site and over 2,000 nearby properties were damaged. The incident occurred at a weekend and the casualty rate among the workers might have been far worse had it occurred on a normal working day.

The plant had previously been shut down when a crack was discovered in one of the reactors. A decision was taken to bypass the reactor so that the plant could

The explosion at Flixborough, Lincolnshire, in 1974

continue production. This modification occurred without a full assessment of the potential consequences.

The investigation raised questions about plant modification without full assessment of the potential consequences, the need for pressure testing during recommissioning, plant layout – including positioning of the control room (where 18 of the workers had been killed) – and emergency planning.

A public inquiry led to the establishment of a Major Hazards Advisory Committee and recommendations for the control of major hazards. A framework of regulatory controls for major hazard plants was subsequently developed in the UK and later in Europe.

Seveso, Italy, 1976

No one died but many people became ill after a cloud of vapour containing dioxin escaped from the Icsema Chemical Company near Seveso, a town of 17,000 inhabitants. The leak was caused by the rupture of a bursting disc on a chemical reactor vessel during an exothermic reaction.

Communication between the company and the authorities was poor, there was a lack of information and there was some confusion about what had happened for some time afterwards.

This event and other major hazard accidents in the European chemical industry, such as at Flixborough (see above), led to the development of Directives for the control of major hazards, known as the Seveso Directives.

Three Mile Island, Harrisburg, Pennsylvania, USA, 1979

The main feedwater pumps at the Three Mile Island nuclear power plant's TMI 1 reactor failed, causing a reduction in the flow of coolant to steam generators. This caused the reactor to shut down automatically. Pressure began to increase and a relief valve opened, but operators were misled by instruments falsely showing that the valve was closed. Pressure began to decrease but the operators were unaware of the loss of coolant and the need to replace it. The top of the reactor core became exposed and the temperature increased with consequential damage to other parts of the system. The controllers watching the instruments still could not work out what was happening. It was not until manual readings from thermocouples revealed the nature of the problem that remedial action was taken, and not before there had been serious damage to the reactor core, releasing large amounts of radioactivity.

The incident revealed problems arising from human reactions and confusion in the face of overwhelming and inaccurate information from instrumentation. Training of staff was focused thereafter on the fundamental issue of ensuring that the core was always receiving enough coolant.

Bhopal, India, 1984

Over 2,000 people died from exposure to fumes, and over 300,000 were injured, soon after an incident at a Union Carbide chemical works surrounded by a shanty town. A relief valve on a storage tank lifted and released methyl isocyanate into the atmosphere. Many more died later and thousands were injured and suffered long-term damage to their health.

Design, maintenance and operational problems involving plant modification and change management were factors contributing to the event. The pressure inside the tank had risen rapidly after unwanted water entering the tank caused an exothermic reaction with the process fluid. The flare system which might have mitigated the effects had been out of action for some time, and plant modification had taken place without full regard to consequences, including the decommissioning of a refrigeration system for keeping the contents of the storage tank at low temperature.

Mexico, 1984

A state-owned PEMEX LPG terminal in Mexico City was destroyed and 500 people were killed in a major fire and series of explosions. The plant was being refilled with gas from a refinery 400km away when a drop in pressure was noticed by the control room and at a pipeline pumping station. Unknown to the operators, a pipe had ruptured between a storage sphere and cylinders, releasing a huge gas cloud. This release continued for several minutes before it found an ignition source and exploded, causing numerous fires and BLEVEs (boiling liquid expanding vapour explosions) as more LPG vessels exploded during the next 90 minutes.

The fire water system was disabled by the initial blast and water spray systems were found to be inadequate. There was a delay in operating the emergency isolating equipment and shutting down the plant. The incident also raised questions about plant layout and positioning of vessels, effective isolation measures in emergency, gas detection systems and emergency planning.

Abbeystead, England, 1984

A methane gas explosion in an underground water valve house station killed 16 and injured 28 members of the public visiting the works. The gas had entered a tunnel pipeline system entrained in water and had gathered, unbeknownst to anyone, in a chamber where the visitors were standing.

The system had been built to transfer water between two river catchments in an area of great natural beauty and the valve house had been sited below ground for environmental reasons. The methane risk had not been foreseen. Design and operational shortcomings were identified by an official investigation.

Bradford, England, 1985

Fifty-six spectators were burnt to death at Bradford City Football Club's ground when a wooden stand, beneath which flammable rubbish had been allowed to accumulate over the years, caught fire. A public inquiry led by Mr Justice Popplewell was followed by a civil action in which the club and various authorities deemed to have allowed the situation to arise were sued for compensation.

The Bradford FC fire was followed soon afterwards by another football tragedy at the Heysel Stadium in Belgium, when a wall separating rival fans collapsed, killing 39 people. The Popplewell Report took this into account and Parliament responded by replacing the Safety of Sports Grounds Act 1975 with the Fire Safety and Safety of Places of Sports Act 1987, supported by a revision of the 'Green Guide' issued by the Home Office.

Later, the Taylor Report of the inquiry into the crowd disaster at Sheffield Wednesday's Hillsborough stadium in 1989, where 96 fans were crushed to death against fencing while others were trying to press into the ground, would recommend that stadia should become all-seated, with no fencing in front of fans.

Chernobyl, USSR, 1986

The radioactive plume released from the Chernobyl nuclear plant near Kiev in Ukraine was first detected in Sweden after it had drifted across Northern Europe. Some 200,000 people in the USSR are believed to have been evacuated and resettled as a result of the worst nuclear accident ever to have occurred.

It was caused when the RBMK type reactor Chernobyl 4 suffered a catastrophic steam explosion, causing further explosions, fires and the eventual destruction of the plant. The safety of this reactor's design was flawed but problems were compounded by attempting to run an experimental test, during which the reactor was allowed by insufficiently trained and informed operating staff to go into an unstable condition. The reactor overheated, fuel rods became jammed and the crisis went out of control. Considerable amounts of radioactive fuel escaped into

The aftermath of the explosion at Chernobyl's Reactor No. 4 in 1986. The entire reactor is now encased in a thick concrete sarcophagus

the atmosphere. Many of the personnel who attempted to bring the incident under control died from exposure to heavy doses of radioactivity. Today the plant remains entombed in a hastily constructed concrete sarcophagus.

This disaster and other incidents such as that at Three Mile Island have had a hugely damaging effect on public perception of the safety of nuclear power generation.

Challenger Space Shuttle, USA, 1986
There was great pressure to go ahead with a launch after delays had occurred for a variety of reasons, including forecasts of bad weather in Florida which proved

to be incorrect. However, very low temperatures during the night before the planned launch gravely concerned the engineers responsible for making the booster rockets. They believed that there was evidence that O-ring seals between booster sections could fail due to exposure to low temperatures and release rocket fuel during take-off, with catastrophic results.

Managers decided that the launch should take place in spite of the engineers' advice. The rest is history.

King's Cross Underground fire, London, 1987

Although smoking had recently been banned on the Underground following a previous fire at Oxford Circus station, a discarded match or cigarette end is believed to have ignited rubbish that had gathered in the escalator machinery beneath the moving staircase leading from the ticket hall to platforms at King's Cross underground station. For a short while the fire was believed to be minor and staff responded accordingly. Members of the public were still entering the station when smoke and flames suddenly roared up the inclined shaft to the ticket office area, killing 31 people.

A public inquiry led by Mr Desmond Fennell QC identified the phenomenon of the fire's behaviour as a 'trench effect' and made numerous recommendations leading, among other provisions, to the replacement of wooden escalators and much stricter observation of the no smoking rule.

Zeebrugge, Belgium, 1987

The cross-Channel ferry *Herald of Free Enterprise* capsized after leaving the port of Zeebrugge with its bow door open, causing the car decks to flood. One hundred and eighty-eight people lost their lives.

The devastated ticket hall at King's Cross Underground station after the 1987 fire

Investigation revealed problems of safety culture and management in the failure of any system for ensuring that the bow door was closed before leaving port. Nevertheless, an attempt to prosecute the ferry operator for corporate manslaughter failed, because of the difficulty encountered in proving a connection between the company's 'directing mind' and the failures of the crew that day.

Other attempts to prosecute cases of 'corporate manslaughter' also failed, causing outrage. However, it would be 20 years before Parliament strengthened the law with the aim of enabling such prosecutions to succeed, when it passed the Corporate Manslaughter and Corporate Homicide Act 2007.

Exxon Valdez, Alaska, USA, 1989

The oil tanker *Exxon Valdez* ran aground in Prince William Sound, Alaska, spilling 11 million gallons of crude oil into the sea. This caused widespread environmental damage and necessitated a huge and costly clean-up operation.

The incident revealed problems in the design of tanker hulls and in communications between vessel captains and vessel traffic controllers. It prompted Congress to pass the Oil Pollution Act 1990, requiring the US Coast Guard to strengthen its regulations on oil tank vessels, owners and operators.

Piper Alpha, North Sea, UK, 1989

In the worst incident of the UK offshore industry's history, 167 men were killed and Occidental's oil platform was destroyed in an explosion and fire after a leak of hydrocarbons. Root causes included faulty maintenance due to inexperience, and poor procedures leading to failures in the fire protection and fighting systems.

Lord Cullen's inquiry into the causes of the disaster made numerous recommendations, including the introduction of a new safety regulatory regime, which requires designers and operators of offshore installations to submit safety cases for acceptance by the regulatory authority.

Lyme Bay, England, 1993

Four teenage pupils were drowned when their canoes were capsized by heavy seas, which had been mounting since they left the shore. Other members of their party, including their teacher and two instructors from the adventure activity company in charge of their expedition, were rescued by the emergency services.

Investigation exposed serious failings in provision of equipment, competence of staff, instruction and supervision. The adventure activity company responsible for organising their trip, and its managing director, were prosecuted and convicted. The director was sentenced to three years' imprisonment for manslaughter.

The tragedy led to tighter regulation and the establishment of the Adventure Activities Licensing Authority.

Heathrow tunnel collapse, London, 1994

Tunnels being built beneath Heathrow Airport collapsed after failures in construction using the New Austrian Tunnelling Method. Fortunately there was time to evacuate the workmen and no one was killed, but the incident caused major short-term disruption to the airport, with significant economic consequences.

The investigation exposed failures in safety management. The main tunnelling contractor was fined £1.2 million with £100,000 costs for offences under health and safety law.

Milford Haven, Wales, 1994

A lightning strike at a refinery during a severe electrical storm started a fire on leaking pipework containing hydrocarbons in process. Part of the plant was shut down in response but an explosion occurred five hours later, followed by a domino effect of further explosions, fires and extensive plant damage. Fortunately no one was killed but 26 workers were injured. It was said that 10 per cent of the UK's oil refining capacity was lost for several months.

The investigation found root causes of the incident in failures of management, equipment and control systems. The operating companies were fined £200,000

The aftermath of the fire at the Texaco oil refinery at Milford Haven in 1994

with £143,700 costs for breaches of health and safety law, but the total cost of the incident was estimated to have exceeded £100 million.

Port Ramsgate, England, 1994

Six members of the public died and seven were seriously injured in the collapse of a pedestrian walkway to a ferry. The collapse occurred because of faulty design and installation. The operating company, the inspection body and the two Swedish companies which designed and constructed the walkway were fined £1.7 million and £723,500 costs. The Swedish companies went bankrupt and never paid the fines.

The collapsed walkway at Port Ramsgate, 1994

Channel Tunnel fire, 1996

A shuttle train carrying truck trailers stopped halfway from France to England when a fire was discovered on board. Passengers were evacuated to another train in an adjacent tunnel without any loss of life, thanks to the safe design of the tunnel system and the response of safety crews from both France and England. The fire, which reached a very high temperature, was put out but not before serious damage had been done to the tunnel lining, estimated at £200 million.

The operators were criticised by the Channel Tunnel Safety Authority's report of its investigation into the fire. This pointed out fundamental weaknesses in emergency preparedness, in that the staff were unable to carry out the emergency procedures, which were too complex and demanding and for which they had not been adequately trained. The authority added that greater attention to rehearsing the procedures would have shown up the undue demands imposed on control room staff.

Paddington, London, 1999

A local train collided head-on with a high-speed train at Ladbroke Grove outside Paddington station after passing a signal at danger (SPAD) and being routed into the path of the oncoming express. Diesel fuel ignited and the trains caught fire. Thirty-one people were killed and over 400 were injured.

An inquiry into the disaster led by Lord Cullen found there had been persistent problems in observing the signal concerned. Among numerous recommendations, he repeated the Hidden Report's recommendation after the Clapham Junction accident of 1988 for the installation of an automatic train protection system. In spite of this and other SPAD disasters (such as at Southall in 1997, where seven people died), the system has been judged too costly to install.

Enschede, Holland, 2000

Around 100 tonnes of explosives blew up at a fireworks warehouse located in a residential district of Enschede, a small town in northern Holland, killing 22 people and injuring 947. The explosion destroyed 400 nearby apartments and damaged 1,000 more. Asbestos is believed to have been released into the atmosphere from blazing buildings.

The owners of the warehouse were convicted, fined and sent to prison for importing and selling illegal fireworks, breaking safety codes and violating storage licences. The court also criticised the authorities for issuing permits to store fireworks in a residential neighbourhood.

Morecambe Bay, England, 2004

At least 21 people employed by gangmasters to gather cockles were drowned when they were trapped on the mudflats in Morecambe Bay by the rapidly incoming tide.

This incident led the government to introduce a new law requiring the licensing of gangmasters under a Gangmasters Licensing Authority. The cocklers' gangmaster was convicted of manslaughter by the Crown Court and sent to prison.

A group of young people on their way to a hiring fair in Lancaster were drowned crossing the same mudflats in 1856.

ICL/Stockline, Scotland, 2004

In the worst industrial disaster in Scotland since Piper Alpha, on 11 May 2004 nine workers were killed and 40 injured when a plastics factory was destroyed by a gas explosion caused by LPG leaking from a corroded underground pipe.

ICL Plastics and ICL Tech pleaded guilty to four offences under the Health and Safety at Work etc Act 1974 and were fined £400,000 at the High Court in Glasgow in 2007. A Public Inquiry has since been held into the causes of the disaster and Lord Gill's report is expected to be published during 2009.

BP, Texas City, USA, 2005

Fifteen people were killed in explosions and fires on 23 March 2005 at BP's refinery at Texas City. Several investigations followed, including one led by the former US Secretary of State, James Baker. BP was fined $21 million for safety breaches by the Occupational Safety and Health Administration and has so far paid out $1.6 billion in compensation.

Buncefield oil depot, England, 2005

Early on Sunday 11 December 2005, thousands of people were awoken by what is said to have been the largest peacetime explosion in the UK – it was heard as far away as Belgium. A highly flammable vapour cloud had formed at a fuel

The Buncefield oil depot fire, 2005 (photo courtesy of Chiltern Air Support Unit)

storage depot after fuel spilled over as a tank was being filled. It is thought that filling continued past the capacity of the tank because a fuel level gauge stuck. The vapour cloud found a source of ignition and exploded, causing further explosions and fires which burned for several days and destroyed the depot.

Miraculously, no-one was killed, even though the site was close to residential and commercial properties, which suffered substantial damage. Over 40 people were injured. Lord Newton's final report of the lengthy investigations was published in December 2008. In July 2010 five companies that had been found guilty of health and safety and environmental offences were fined a total of £9.5 million.

Gulf of Mexico oil spill, 2010

In April 2010 an explosion at the Deepwater Horizon offshore oil installation killed 11 workers and resulted in the USA's worst environmental disaster. Millions of barrels of crude oil escaped into the Gulf of Mexico from the damaged well before it was successfully capped. Clean-up operations and investigations are continuing.

References and further reading

This chapter gives a brief explanation of some of the highest-profile disasters of the last half-century. Many more over the last 200 years are explored at greater depth in *Disasters: learning the lessons for a safer world* by David Eves, published by IOSH in 2010.

Aberfan, 1966

Davies E (chairman). *Report of the Tribunal appointed to inquire into the disaster at Aberfan on October 21st 1966*, HL 316, HC 553 (HMSO, London, 1967; pp.131–132)

Feyzin, 1966

HSE. *Refinery fire at Feyzin*, 4 January 1966 (HSE website, www.hse.gov.uk, 2004)

Lees F P. Loss prevention in the process industries – hazard identification, assessment and control, vol.3, appendix 1 (Butterworth Heinemann, 1996)

Flixborough, 1974

HSE. *The Flixborough disaster: report of the Court of Inquiry* (HMSO, London, 1975)

Seveso, 1976

Lees F P. *Loss prevention in the process industries – hazard identification, assessment and control*, vol.3, appendix 3 (Butterworth Heinemann, 1996)

Three Mile Island, 1979

Sills D L, Wolf C P and Shelanski V B. *Accident at Three Mile Island: the human dimensions* (Westview Press, Boulder, Colorado, 1982)

Bhopal, 1984

Lees F P. *Loss prevention in the process industries – hazard identification, assessment and control*, vol.3, appendix 5 (Butterworth Heinemann, 1996)

Mexico, 1984

Lees F P. *Loss prevention in the process industries – hazard identification, assessment and control*, vol.3, appendix 4 (Butterworth Heinemann, 1996)

Marsh and McLennan. *Large property damage losses in the hydrocarbon–chemical industries: a thirty-year review*, 16th edition (Marsh and McLennan Protection Consultants, 1995)

Abbeystead, 1984

HSE. *The Abbeystead explosion: a report of the investigation by the HSE into the explosion on 23 May 1984 at the valve house of the Lune/Wyre Water Transfer Scheme at Abbeystead* (HSE Books, Sudbury, 1985)

Bradford, 1985

Popplewell, Lord Justice. *Committee of inquiry into crowd safety and control at sports grounds – final report*, Cmnd 9710 (HMSO, London, 1986)

Taylor, Lord Justice. *The Hillsborough Stadium disaster, 15 April 1989 – final report* (HMSO, London, 1990)

Department of National Heritage, Scottish Office. *Guide to safety at sports grounds* (Green Guide, 4th edition) (HMSO, London, 1997)

Challenger Space Shuttle, 1986

National Aeronautics and Space Agency. *Report of the Presidential Commission on the Space Shuttle Challenger accident*, science.ksc.nasa.gov/shuttle/missions/51-l/docs/rogers-commission/table-of-contents.html

Chernobyl, 1986

Hawkes N, Lean G, Leigh D, McKie R, Pringle P and Wilson A. *The worst accident in the world. Chernobyl: the end of the nuclear dream* (Pan Books Ltd, London, 1986)

Chernobyl nuclear disaster website, www.chernobyl.co.uk

King's Cross, 1987

Fennell D. *Investigation into the King's Cross Underground fire*, presented to Parliament by the Secretary of State for Transport (HMSO, London, 1988)

Zeebrugge, 1987

Sheen, Mr Justice. *MV Herald of Free Enterprise*. Report of Court No.8074. Formal
   investigation (Department of Transport, London, 1987)

Exxon Valdez, 1989

Oil Program, US Environmental Protection Agency website, www.epa.gov/oilspill/exxon.htm

Piper Alpha, 1989

Cullen, Lord. *The Public Inquiry into the Piper Alpha disaster* (HMSO, London, 1990)

Lyme Bay, 1993

Adventure Activities Licensing Authority website, www.aala.org/lymebay01.html

Heathrow Tunnel, 1994

HSE. *A report on the investigation by the HSE into the collapse of the New Austrian
   Tunnelling Method (NATM) tunnels at the Central Terminal Area of Heathrow on
   20/21 October 1994* (HSE Books, Sudbury, 2000)

Milford Haven, 1994

Fewtrell P and Hirst I L. 'A review of high-cost chemical/petrochemical accidents since
   1974' (*IChemE Loss Prevention Bulletin*, 140, pp.1–12)

HSE. *A report of the investigation by the HSE into the explosion and fires on the
   Pembroke Cracking Company plant at the Texaco Refinery, Milford Haven, on 24 July
   1994* (HSE Books, Sudbury, 1997)

Port Ramsgate, 1994

HSE. *A report on the investigation into the walkway collapse at Port Ramsgate on 14
   September 1994* (HSE Books, Sudbury, 2000)

Channel Tunnel Fire, 1986

Department of Transport. *Inquiry into the fire on the heavy goods vehicle shuttle 7539 on 18 November 1996* (DfT website, www.dft.gov.uk/stellent/groups/dft_railways/ documents/page/dft_railways_504363-02.hcsp)

Paddington, 1999

HSE. *The train collision at Ladbroke Grove on 5 October 1999: a report of the HSE investigation* (HSE Books, Sudbury, 2000)

Hidden A. *Investigation into the Clapham Junction railway accident* (HMSO, London, 1989)

Enschede, 2000

Ministry of the Interior and Kingdom Relations Final Report, www.emergency-management.net/enschede1.pdf

Morecambe Bay, 2004

HSE. *Guidelines for safe working in estuaries and tidal areas when harvesting produce such as cockles, mussels and shrimps*, www.hse.gov.uk/pubns/estuary.htm

ICL/Stockline, 2004

The ICL/Stockline disaster, www.hazards.org/icldisaster/fullreport.htm

BP Texas City, 2005

US Chemical Safety Board. *BP America refinery explosion*, www.csb.gov/investigations/ detail.aspx?SID=20

The Baker Report is available from BP's website at www.bp.com/liveassets/ bp_internet/globalbp/globalbp_uk_english/reports_and_publications/presentations/ STAGING/local_assets/pdf/Baker_panel_report.pdf

Buncefield, 2005

Official investigation website, www.buncefieldinvestigation.gov.uk, including Lord
    Newton's 2008 final report

Gulf of Mexico, 2010

BP's official oil spill response page, www.bp.com/bodycopyarticle.do?categoryId=
    1&contentId=7052055

Restore the Gulf, the US Government's official website covering efforts to repair the
    damage, www.restorethegulf.gov

Employers' Liability Compulsory Insurance

"The government recognises that too many businesses have faced steep price increases, late renewals and premiums that fail to reflect their health and safety record." *Des Browne, Minister for Work, 4 December 2003*

Employers are bound by law to take out cover known as Employers' Liability Compulsory Insurance (ELCI). Under the Employers' Liability Compulsory Insurance Act 1969 employers are required to insure against any liability for negligence so that they can meet the cost of compensation for employees' injuries or illnesses.

An HSE survey has shown that while the level of compliance with this law is high, many firms struggle to secure insurance on grounds of affordability. The UK's system of compensation for workplace injury and ill health has been creaking badly for some years. Premiums have soared and do not reflect the performance of individual companies. The costs to employers contain a substantial element of legal fees and have become disproportionately high compared with the benefits to workers.

Nearly three decades ago the Pearson Report recommended 'no fault liability' and compensation but this was never acted on. ELCI at present gives little or no incentive to employers to improve health and safety performance or offer rehabilitation to injured workers. The government has recently undertaken a review of the whole spectrum of current employers' liability and arrangements for compensation of injured workers.

The Department of Work and Pensions report of the Second Stage of the ELCI Review (2004) proposes these 'workable solutions':

- publication of a new 'framework of vocational rehabilitation'
- the possibility of fixed-fee schemes for employers' liability

- collaborating with insurers, business and the HSE to develop an approach to underwriting that reflects individual firms' health and safety performance.

For the time being your company must at the very least have Employers' Liability Compulsory Insurance under the existing ELCI legislation and display a valid certificate of insurance.

The law is enforced by the HSE and its inspectors (including its Workplace Contact Officers, Working Time Officers and Compliance Officers) may ask to see the certificate. If this cannot be produced, the HSE will usually write to the employer and if a certificate is not then produced they will serve a 'notice to produce'. Failure then to produce a valid certificate is an offence for which the employer may be prosecuted. Penalties are up to £2,500 for each day on which employers are without insurance and up to £1,000 for failure to display or produce a certificate.

There are ideas under consideration about passing on the costs of NHS treatment for staff injured or made ill by their work to their employers. Consultation on draft regulations for a new, expanded NHS Injury Costs Recovery scheme took place in 2004. The government is considering the issues and concerns raised by stakeholders in the consultation and, as a result, the planned introduction of new regulations in April 2005 has been postponed, probably until autumn 2006. Hospitals are already able to recover the costs of treating people injured in road traffic accidents, which is currently (2003/04) estimated to be recovering £116 million per year for the NHS. It is expected that the expanded scheme will recover a similar amount per year, and that employers who face these costs will be encouraged to take steps to avoid injuries to their employees.

References and further reading

Department of Health. The recovery of National Health Service costs in cases involving personal injury compensation: a consultation (DoH website, www.dh.gov.uk, 2005)

Department of Work and Pensions. *Review of Employers' Liability Insurance: second stage report*, ELCI 2 (DWP website, www.dwp.gov.uk, 2004)

Employers' Liability Compulsory Insurance Act 1969

Pearson, Lord. *Report on the Royal Commission on civil liability and compensation for personal injury* (HMSO, London, 1978)

Wright M, Marsden S, Turner D and Genna R. *Survey of compliance with the Employers' Liability Compulsory Insurance (ELCI) Act 1969*, RR188 (HSE website, www.hse.gov.uk/research/rrpdf/rr.188.pdf, 2003)

Government strategies, targets and priorities

Directors are advised to keep up to date with the government's aspirations for health and safety at work

Government strategies and initiatives

National targets for improving health and safety at work over 10 years were set by the government in documents published in 2000 called 'Revitalising health and safety at work' and 'Securing health together'.

National targets for 2000–2010

The targets are:

- 30 per cent reduction in rate of working days lost per 100,000 workers through work-related illness and injury
- 20 per cent reduction in the incidence rate of work-related ill health
- 10 per cent reduction in the incidence rate of work-related fatal and major injuries.

(The incidence rate is the number of injuries or cases of ill health per 100,000 workers.)

The government aimed at achieving half of these targets by 2004 but this has proved unrealistic.

Some industrial sectors have set and taken 'ownership' of their own targets for improvement. The relevant trade associations should be contacted for information about these. Directors might consider setting targets in their companies.

HSE priorities

A new strategy for achieving the national targets was published in 2004 (see below, 'Strategy for workplace health and safety in Great Britain to 2010 and beyond'). Eight priority areas were identified where improvement is most needed to achieve these targets:

- construction
- agriculture
- the health service
- work-related stress
- musculoskeletal disorders
- falls from height
- slips and trips
- work-related transport.

A ninth has since been added:

- government setting an example.

Some recent strategies

The HSC published a new 'Strategy for workplace health and safety in Great Britain to 2010 and beyond' in February 2004, when it was becoming clear that progress towards the national targets would not be realised.

In 2004, the European Commission also revisited its strategic objectives for workplace health and safety, rolling them forward for the period 2005–09.

In late 2005, another 'overarching' strategy called 'Health, work and well-being –

caring for our future' was announced by the Department of Work and Pensions, Department for Health and the HSE. Professor Dame Carol Black has been appointed as the first National Director for Health and Work with the aim of co-ordinating government efforts to improve health, a strategy first announced in 'Our healthier nation'. A review of the working age population's health, entitled 'Working for a healthier tomorrow', was published in March 2008.

In 'The Health and Safety Executive business plan for 2008/09', Judith Hackitt, chair of the HSE, reported that the picture on targets was 'mixed': the statistics for 2006/07 showed that the HSE's work was on track to deliver the government's injury targets under the Department for Work and Pensions' Public Service Agreement, but there was more to be done to meet the ill health and lost working days targets.

In June 2009, the HSE launched another new strategy, 'The health and safety of Great Britain: Be part of the solution'. Acknowledging that the regulatory authorities cannot deliver improved health and safety performance on their own, the HSE has invited companies and organisations to sign up to a strategy that sets 'goals' rather than targets, with the aim of encouraging:

- strong leadership
- a common sense approach
- building competence
- workforce involvement
- healthier and safer workplaces
- customised support for small businesses
- better avoidance of catastrophes.

HSE programmes

In support of its strategy and the targets for 2010, the HSE has pursued:

- priority programmes
- major hazard industries
- securing compliance with the law
- mandatory activities.

A company may well find itself subject to the HSE's compliance programme but may also attract its attention in other areas.

To carry out these programmes, the HSE has about 3,500 staff, including around 1,500 inspectors carrying out enforcement duties. There are also scientists, engineers, medical and other experts on the payroll. The HSE's budget is currently about £240 million, mainly staff-related. Local authorities employ the equivalent of about 1,100 full time inspectors (normally environmental health officers who include health and safety enforcement in their wider role).

The HSE's and local authorities' main work of securing compliance is free to businesses, but the HSE charges for certain activities such as safety case assessment.

The Health and Safety Laboratory, based at Buxton, is an agency of the HSE and has a separate budget for conducting research and forensic investigations. Its chief customer is the HSE but it is able to bid for work elsewhere, including the private sector.

Enforcement, offences and penalties

The Regulatory Enforcement and Sanctions Act was passed by Parliament in 2008. Part of the government's 'Better Regulation' agenda, it aims to improve and simplify the way legislation is made and enforced, based on the general principle that enforcement should focus on where the risks are greatest.

The HSE already follows this principle. Responsibility for health and safety enforcement is shared by the HSE with the 400 or so local authorities in Great Britain and is divided between them according to sector and activity. The HSE makes about 200,000 'regulatory contacts' a year, including inspections and investigations. Local authorities pay more visits but use the same methods – checking compliance, giving advice and investigating complaints and serious accidents.

In 2007/08 the HSE issued 7,740 enforcement notices (improvements and prohibitions), compared to 8,274 in 2006/07. If local authorities' enforcement activities are added, the national total approaches 15,000.

The HSE prosecuted 1,137 offences in 2007/08, completing 1,028, for which 839 convictions were secured (a conviction rate of 82 per cent). As multiple offences are prosecuted in some cases, the total of 1,028 represents only 565 prosecutions against employers. The average penalty per offence was £12,896, but if untypical penalties exceeding £100,000 are excluded, this drops to £7,809.

Local authorities prosecuted 354 offences, resulting in 334 convictions (a rate of 95 per cent). The average fine was £5,560 if untypical large fines are omitted.

There has recently been a trend towards much higher fines. In 2005 a Scottish judge imposed a £15 million fine after a leak from a gas main killed four members of the public. A fine of £10 million, reduced on appeal to £7.5 million, was imposed after the Hatfield train crash. In 2006, a fine of £1.3 million was imposed after a blast furnace explosion at a Welsh steelworks in 2001 that killed three workers. In 2010, five companies were fined a total of £9.5 million in connection with the disaster at Buncefield.

References and further reading

DWP, DH, HSE. *Health, work and well-being – caring for our future* (DWP website, www.dwp.gov.uk, 2005)

HSC. *Strategy for workplace health and safety in Great Britain to 2010 and beyond* (HSE website, www.hse.gov.uk, 2004)

HSE. *Health and safety offences and penalties 2004/2005, a report by the Health and Safety Executive* (HSE website, www.hse.gov.uk, 2005)

HSE. *Revitalising health and safety* (HSE website, www.hse.gov.uk, 2000)

HSE. *Securing health together* (HSE website, www.hse.gov.uk, 2000)

Injury and ill health statistics

The information below has been extracted from databases maintained by the HSE, the EU and the ILO

Fatalities in Great Britain in 2010/11

Great Britain has one of the lowest rates of fatal injury in Europe. In 2010/11:

- 171 fatal injuries (provisional figure) occurred to workers (147 in 2009/10, 180 in 2008/09, 233 in 2007/08); the fatal injury rate was 0.6 per 100,000 workers

Injuries in 2009/10

- There were 233,000 (HSE estimate) injuries such as amputations, burns or fractures.

Working days lost from accidents and ill health in 2009/10

- 28.5 million days were lost, 23.4 million due to work-related ill health and 5.1 million due to workplace injury (estimates from the Labour Force Survey)

Ill health statistics

The most common types of work-related illness in Britain are:

- musculoskeletal disorders
- mental ill health (mainly stress, depression and anxiety).

In addition, the HSE estimated that 12,000 ill health deaths occur each year resulting from past occupational exposure:

- cancer – 8,000 deaths from past exposure to carcinogens
- chronic obstructive pulmonary disease (COPD) – 4,000 deaths from past occupational exposure to fumes, chemicals and dust

The HSE estimated that in 2007/08:

- 2.1 million people suffered from ill health which they thought was work-related (2.2 million in 2006/07, 2 million in 2005/06)
- two-thirds of cases of ill health were musculoskeletal disorders or stress.

(From figures published by the HSE in 2008.)

European Union statistics

Before the enlargement of the EU in 2004, EU statistical sources estimate that every year in the 15 member states:

- 4,900 people are killed in workplace accidents
- almost 1,200 of these are construction workers
- over 4.7 million workplace accidents occur
- 5,900 people die of occupational diseases
- around 210 million working days are lost
- this costs the construction sector alone €75 billion a year
- of that, €20 billion a year is a result of direct insurance costs alone.

At the time of writing, statistics have not been published for the 25 member states of the enlarged EU.

Global statistics

Global figures are even harder to come by. The International Labour Organization estimates that over 2 million workers die each year from work-related accidents and diseases, and 250 million are injured.

An indication of the ILO's global priorities for improving working conditions is to be found in 'Decent work', a report produced in 1999, and the ILO Declaration on Fundamental Principles and Rights at Work. Adopted in 1998, the Declaration is an expression of commitment by governments and employers' and workers' organisations to uphold basic human values. It covers four areas:

- freedom of association and the right to collective bargaining
- elimination of forced and compulsory labour
- effective abolition of child labour
- elimination of discrimination in the workplace.

References and further reading

Eurostat: epp.eurostat.cec.eu.int/portal/page?_pageid=1090,1137397&_dad=
portal&_schema=PORTAL

HSE. *Health and safety statistics 2007/08* (HSE website, www.hse.gov.uk)

HSE. *The self-reported work-related illness (SWI) survey 2004/05* (HSE website,
www.hse.gov.uk)

International Labour Organization website, www.ilo.org

International Labour Organization. *Decent work* (ILO website, www.ilo.org/public/
english/standards/relm/ilc/ilc87/rep-i.htm, 1999)

International Labour Organization. *Declaration on fundamental principles and rights
at work* (ILO, Geneva, 1998)

Some key standards and guidance

There is a vast quantity of national and international standards and published guidance. Here are a few key organisations, standards and publications that are worth knowing about

Standards

Directors should be aware of the following:

Standard-making organisations

- BSI (British Standards Institution, www.bsi-global.com)
- CEN (European Committee for Standardization, www.cenorm.be)
- CENELEC (European Committee for Electrotechnical Standardization, www.cenelec.org)
- ISO (International Organization for Standardization, www.iso.org)
- ILO (International Labour Organization, www.ilo.org)

Some key standards

- ISO 9000 series (quality management)
- ISO 14000 series (environmental management)
- BS EN ISO 19011 (guidelines for quality and/or environmental management systems auditing)
- BS 8555 (environmental management systems)
- BS 18004 (guide to occupational health and safety management)
- OHSAS 18001 (occupational health and safety)
- ILO Occupational safety and health management systems guidelines

Guidance

The director may find it worth keeping a few publications to hand:

HSE. *Essentials of health and safety at work* (HSE Books, Sudbury, 1999)

HSE. *Successful health and safety management*, HSG65 (HSE Books, Sudbury, 2000)

Hyde P and Reeve P. *Essentials of environmental management* (IOSH Services, Leicester, 2004)

HSE. *Five steps to risk assessment* (HSE Books, Sudbury, 1999; free PDF available from www.hse.gsi.gov.uk)

Institute of Directors and HSC, free leaflet. *Leading health and safety at work*, INDG417, (HSE Books, Sudbury, 2007)

Some useful sources of information

There are numerous sources of health, safety and environmental information. The list that follows is not exhaustive but includes a number of organisations that a director could find helpful, depending on the problem that needs to be explored.

Association of Occupational Health Nurse Practitioners: www.aohnp.co.uk

British Occupational Hygiene Society: www.bohs.org

British Safety Council: www.britishsafetycouncil.co.uk

British Standards Institution: www.bsi-global.com

Chartered Institute of Personnel and Development: www.cipd.co.uk

Chartered Institute of Environmental Health: www.cieh.org

Confederation of British Industry: www.cbi.org.uk

Consumers' Association: www.which.net

CSR.gov.uk: UK government gateway to corporate social responsibility: www.societyandbusiness.gov.uk

Department for the Environment, Food and Rural Affairs: www.defra.gov.uk

Department of Health: www.dh.gov.uk

Department of Trade and Industry: www.dti.gov.uk

Department for Transport: www.dft.gov.uk

Department for Work and Pensions: www.dwp.gov.uk

Disability Rights Commission: www.drc-gb.org

Engineering Employers Federation: www.eef.org.uk

Environment Agency: www.environment-agency.gov.uk

Ergonomics Society: www.ergonomics.org.uk

Eurostat: epp.eurostat.cec.eu.int

European Agency for Safety and Health at Work, Bilbao: europe.osha.eu.int

Faculty of Occupational Medicine: www.facoccmed.ac.uk

Fire Protection Association: www.thefpa.co.uk

Health and Safety Executive: www.hse.gov.uk

Health Protection Agency: www.hpa.org.uk

HSE Infoline: 0845 345 0055

HSE Books: PO Box 1999, Sudbury, Suffolk CO10 2WA

Institute of Directors: www.iod.com

Institute of Occupational and Environmental Medicine (at the University of Birmingham): www.pcpoh.bham.ac.uk/ioem/

Institution of Occupational Safety and Health: www.iosh.co.uk

International Institute of Risk and Safety Management: www.iirsm.org

International Labour Organization: www.ilo.org

International Organization for Standardization: www.iso.org

Ministry of Justice: www.justice.gov.uk/guidance/manslaughter

National Radiological Protection Board: see Health Protection Agency

Office of Public Sector Information: www.opsi.gov.uk (contains text of all Acts of Parliament and Statutory Instruments since 1987)

Office of the Deputy Prime Minister: www.odpm.gov.uk

Royal College of Nursing: www.rcn.org.uk

Royal Society for the Prevention of Accidents: www.rospa.org.uk

Scottish Environmental Protection Agency: www.sepa.org.uk

Society of Occupational Medicine: www.som.org.uk

Suzy Lamplugh Trust: www.suzylamplugh.org

Trades Union Congress: www.tuc.org.uk

Glossary

Directors won't want to allow themselves to be bamboozled by experts' jargon and should demand an explanation if they don't understand what they are being told. Here are a few of the acronyms, buzz words and mantras which commonly crop up in discussions about health, safety, quality or the environment.

ACOP	approved code of practice, ie approved by the HSC
ALARA	as low as reasonably achievable
ALARP	as low as reasonably practicable
Auditing	process of systematic checking that management systems are in place and effective
Aversion factor	a hazard that could cause multiple deaths and therefore public dismay will sometimes lead experts to apply an 'aversion factor', effectively increasing the amount of effort (time, cost, trouble) that should be taken to reduce risk 'as low as reasonably practicable'
BAT	best available technology
BATNEEC	best available technology not entailing excessive cost
BLEVE	boiling liquid expanding vapour explosion
BPEO	best practicable environmental option
CAWR	Control of Asbestos at Work Regulations
CBA	cost–benefit analysis, used in conjunction with a quantified risk assessment to provide economic justification for risk reduction – see QRA
CDM	Construction (Design and Management) Regulations
CER	Corporate environmental report

Certification to a standard	achieving third party recognition of compliance with a standard, eg to ISO 14001
CMCHA	Corporate Manslaughter and Corporate Homicide Act 2007
COSHH	Control of Substances Hazardous to Health Regulations
CSR	corporate social responsibility
DSE	display screen equipment
Duty holder	policy makers' term for someone with statutory duties and responsibilities
EMAS	environmental management systems audit or employment medical advisory service
EMS	environmental management system
EPIs	environmental performance indicators
GMO	genetically modified organism
GRI	Global Reporting Initiative
HASWA	Health and Safety at Work etc Act 1974
Hazard	something with potential to cause harm
HAZOP	hazards and operability study
High hazard industries	eg chemicals, petroleum, nuclear, offshore oil and gas
HSEQ	health, safety, environment, quality
Incidence rate	in official statistics for the incidence of fatal accidents, the number of accidents per 100,000 workers
Inherently safer design	getting design right in the first place can often lead to a safer outcome. It is more difficult and expensive to retrofit safety
IPPC	Integrated Pollution Prevention and Control (EU Directive)
KPIs	key performance indicators
KSI	key survival issue

LOLER	Lifting Operations and Lifting Equipment Regulations
Method statement	written explanation of how a hazardous process is to be carried out, eg demolition of a building
MSD	musculoskeletal disorder
Permissioning regime	regulatory system in which the regulator permits operation, eg by licensing or acceptance of a safety case, usually for high hazard industries
Permit to work	written authorisation specifying method of work in hazardous situation, eg entry into confined space
Plan, do, check, act	common structure for management systems
POPMAR	set policy, organise, plan, monitor, audit and review: structure for safety, health and environment management system
PPE	personal protective equipment
Precautionary principle	erring on the safe side if uncertain
PSA	probabilistic safety assessment, particularly in the nuclear industry
PUWER	Provision and Use of Work Equipment Regulations
QRA	quantified risk assessment, used with risk matrices and cost benefit analysis to determine compliance with the ALARP principle – see ALARP
Responsible Care	national chemical industry programme for achieving good safety, health and environment performance
Risk	the chance or likelihood of harm being caused by a hazard
Risk assessment	method for identifying hazards, calculating risks, prioritising action
Risk aversion	societal tendency to take more care about risks generally, particularly when dreaded such as cancer, radiation

Risk matrices	method used by QRA experts for scoring or weighting factors in risk assessment to determine priorities for action
Root cause	the underlying cause of an accident, sometimes multiple
RSI	repetitive strain injury
Safety case	written demonstration of assessment of risks, control measures and management systems for achieving safe operation
SAPs	safety assessment principles, particularly in the nuclear industry
SFAIRP	so far as is reasonably practicable
SHE	safety, health and environment
SHEQ	safety, health, environment, quality – see also HSEQ
SMART	targets or objectives which are specific, measurable, agreed, realistic and timebound
SPAD	signal passed at danger (on the railways)
Stakeholders	policy makers' term for anyone with an interest, usually expecting to be consulted
Sustainability	the goal towards which 'sustainable development' leads
Sustainable development	a process leading to sustainability
SWOT analysis	analysis of strengths, weaknesses, opportunities, threats – ie key survival issues
Systems failure	a generic term usually applied to multiple root causes of a failure to manage health and safety rather than to an individual's mistake
The polluter pays	principle of environmental protection law
TOR	tolerability of risk

Uncertainty lack of data in risk assessment, leading to application of the 'precautionary principle'. (It is almost inevitable that there will be uncertainty about some of the data needed to assess a complex risk. The more uncertainty, the greater is the need for a precautionary approach)

What gets measured
  gets done well-known quote from Drucker's management theories
WRULD work-related upper limb disorder

Key Statutes, Regulations and pending Directives

This list points to some of the key legislation relevant to health, safety and the environment but should not be regarded as exhaustive. The HSE implements any changes in either April or October, after consultation has been completed. For detailed, definitive further information, reference should be made to the websites of the Health and Safety Executive, the Environment Agency or the Stationery Office.

Statutes

Clean Air Act 1993

Control of Pollution (Amendment) Act 1989

Corporate Manslaughter and Corporate Homicide Act 2007

Data Protection Act 1998

Disability Discrimination Acts 1995 and 2005

Environment Act 1993

Environmental Protection Act 1990

Freedom of Information Act 2000

Explosives Acts 1875 and 1923

Food and Environment Protection Act 1985

Health and Safety at Work etc Act 1974

Health and Safety (Offences) Act 2008

New Roads and Street Works Act 1991

Pesticides Act 1998

Pollution Prevention and Control Act 1999

Regulatory Enforcement and Sanctions Act 2008

Water Acts 1989 and 2003

Water Resources Act 1991

Health and Safety Regulations

Building Regulations 2000

Carriage of Dangerous Goods and Use of Transportable Pressure Equipment Regulations 2004

Chemicals (Hazard Information and Packaging for Supply) Regulations 2009

Company Directors Disqualification Act 1986

Confined Spaces Regulations 1997

Construction (Design and Management) Regulations 2007

Control of Asbestos Regulations 2006

Control of Lead at Work Regulations 2002 (amended 2004)

Control of Major Accident Hazards Regulations 1999 (amended 2005)

Control of Noise at Work Regulations 2005

Control of Substances Hazardous to Health Regulations 2002 (amended 2004)

Control of Vibration at Work Regulations 2005

Dangerous Substances and Explosive Atmospheres Regulations 2002

Display Screen Equipment Regulations 1992

Electricity at Work Regulations 1989

European Regulation on the Classification, Labelling and Packaging of Substances and Mixtures 2008 (the 'CLP Regulation')

Factories Act 1961 and Offices, Shops and Railway Premises Act 1963 (Repeals and Modifications) Regulations 2009

Health and Safety (Consultation with Employees) Regulations 1996

Health and Safety (First Aid) Regulations 1981

Health and Safety Information (Amendment) Regulations 2009

Health and Safety (Miscellaneous Amendments) Regulations 2002

Health and Safety (Miscellaneous Amendments and Revocations) Regulations 2009

Health and Safety (Safety Signs and Signals) Regulations 1996

Ionising Radiation Regulations 1999

Lifting Operations and Lifting Equipment Regulations 1998

Management of Health and Safety at Work Regulations 1999

Manual Handling Operations Regulations 1992

Manufacture and Storage of Explosives Regulations 2005

Notification of Cooling Towers and Evaporative Condensers Regulations 1992

Notification of New Substances Regulations 1993

Personal Protective Equipment Regulations 1992

Pressure Equipment Regulations 1999

Pressure Systems Safety Regulations 2000

Prohibition of Smoking in Certain Premises (Scotland) Regulations 2006

Provision and Use of Work Equipment Regulations 1998

Radiation (Emergency Preparedness and Public Information) Regulations 2001

Regulatory Reform (Fire Safety) Order 2005

Reporting of Injuries, Diseases and Dangerous Occurrences Regulations 1995

Simple Pressure Vessel (Safety) Regulations 1991 (amended 1994)

Smoke-free (Premises and Enforcement) Regulations 2006 (England only)

Smoke-free Premises etc (Wales) Regulations 2007

Smoking (Northern Ireland) Order 2006

Supply of Machinery (Safety) (Amendment) Regulations 2005

Safety Representatives and Safety Committees Regulations 1977

Work at Height Regulations 2005

Work in Compressed Air Regulations 1996

Working Time Regulations 1998 (amended 2004)

Workplace (Health, Safety and Welfare) Regulations 1992

Environmental regulations

There are even more numerous regulations on environmental matters made under each of the several environmental Acts of Parliament mentioned above. Full details may be found on the Environment Agency's website, www.environment-agency.gov.uk/netregs.

European health and safety Directives pending

The European Commission declared in 2002 that its priority was not to make more health and safety law but to see that existing law was properly implemented. This policy decision has not stemmed the tide so far. The following initiatives are still working through the system and will have to be carried through into UK law in the coming years. The summary below is based on information on the HSE and EC websites in early 2009:

- REACH: a new EC strategy for controlling risks from chemicals. The EU's REACH (Registration, Evaluation, Authorisation and Restriction of Chemicals) Regulation (EC) 1907/2006 came into force on 1 June 2007. It aims to improve the protection of human health and the environment, giving greater responsibility to industry to manage the risks from chemicals and to provide safety information. It will have significant effects on national legislation implementing the strategy.
- Biocidal Products Directive (98/8/EC): establishes a single market in biocidal products. In 2009, the European Commission published proposals for a revision of the Directive that would extend the transitional period for existing active substances from 2010 to 2013.
- Physical Agents (Electromagnetic Fields) Directive (2004/40/EC amended by 2008/46/EC): the date by which this has to be implemented by member states has been extended from 2008 to 2012.

- Physical Agents (Optical Radiation) Directive 2006/25/EC: this directive deals with risks from artificial optical radiation and has to be implemented by April 2010.
- Working Time Directive: regulations controlling the hours of junior doctors came into effect in August 2004 with a five-year transitional period.
- The Globally Harmonised System of Classification and Labelling of Chemicals: the European Commission is seeking to implement the United Nations system of the same name in the EU by means of a draft regulation.

Health and safety regulations in the pipeline

The Hampton Review (2005) recommended that for every new rule, another should be struck out. Nevertheless, regulatory activity continues to add new rules to the statute book. When he reported, the following regulations and changes were working through the system:

- Occupational Exposure Limit (OEL) Framework Revision
- Refractory Ceramics Fibres Workplace Exposure Limit
- Coal Mines (Inhalable Dust) Regulations
- Genetically Modified Organisms (Contained Use) (Amendment) Regulations
- Nuclear Reactors (Environmental Impact Assessment for Decommissioning) (Amendment) Regulations
- Biocidal Products (Amendment) Regulations
- Tank Vehicle (Loading and Unloading of Petroleum Spirit) Regulations
- Management of Health and Safety at Work and Health and Safety (Consultation with Employees) (Amendment) Regulations
- Offshore Installations (Safety Case) Regulations

As a consequence of Hampton and 'Better Regulation' initiatives, the flow of regulations made by the HSE has slowed to a trickle. In 2011 the government launched a 'Red Tape Challenge' in which the public and businesses are invited to suggest which regulations should be kept and which should go, including health and safety regulations. The review should report in the autumn of 2011.

Reference and further reading

Hampton P. *Reducing administrative burdens: effective inspection and enforcement* (HM Treasury, London, 2005)

Index